cover photo: *Cuisine-objet*, project for exhibition “Premices: Invested spaces in visual arts, architecture and design from France, 1958-1998” , Guggenheim Museum , New York.

Computer-generated picture: Pascal Cagninassi (Deis)

editor assistant: Stéphane Argillet

Special Thanks to:

Elsa Douineau, Marianne Min, Patrick Lébedeff, David Gill, Agnès Belbeau-Kentisch et *En Attendant les Barbares*, Lise Gallois et l'*Agence Kréo*, Joseph Holtzman et *Nest magazine*, Antoine Bootz, Thibault Jeanson, Frédéric Basset et *Inside Stock Image Production*, Sophie Hass et *BGH Editions*, Deidi von Schaewen, Eric Bernt et *Résidences magazine*, Annika Hessner-Berner et *Poeform*, Jean-Pierre Godaut, Guy Benhamou, Laure Dupavillon et *Christian Lacroix*, Anita Caudron et *Maffia*, Michael Von Jakubovski et *Best Friends*, Eva-Maria Melchers, *Blome Gmbh*, Joelle Palazon et *Nina Ricci*, Mme Bersani et le Mobilier National, Frederic de Luca, Pascal Cagninacci et *Deis*

3, RUE BEAUTREILLIS
75004 PARIS

ISBN 2-906-571-77-6

PRINTED IN EUROPE

ELIZABETH GAROUSTE & MATTIA BONETTI

this series edited by

PIERRE STAUDENMEYER

in the same series

BOREK SÍPEK

Philippe Louguet, Dagmar Sedlická

RON ARAD

Raymond Guidot, Olivier Boissière

ANDREA BRANZI

François Burkhardt, Cristina Morozzi

ELIZABETH GAROUSTE & MATTIA BONETTI

PIERRE STAUDENMEYER

NADIA CROQUET

LAURENT LE BON

CONTENTS

Climax Credo

Delenda est Such could well have been the rallying cry, celebrating as it does the passing of a thoroughly ideological modernism—however marked by fashion phenomena such as late 1970s conceptual mannerism or the industrial recuperation thought of as the 'high tech' of the day—which united both snobbish and more cultured enthusiasts of the primitivism which launched the Garouste and Bonetti pair on the French design scene.

It was in 1982 that the famous decorating house Jansen, run at the time by Jeanne Gambert de Loche, offered one of their floors on the rue Royale for the two creators to show their "barbarities", after Gérard Garouste had introduced them to the decoration concept of the Privilege—the underground and resuscitated extension of the Palace, very much in vogue at the time. Patinated wrought iron, calf or foal hide, rocaille-shaped or female callipygian-shaped 'papier-mâché', rough or stained oak, rope rigging: such were some of the raw materials Garouste and Bonetti used to express their firm opposition both to the ascepticized and monochromatic world of creation at that time—which has become 'industrial' since the establishment of the Centre de création industrielle—and to the black-and-white radical chic which reigned supreme in the world of decoration. It was also to a form primitivism, that of the high Middle Ages, or even that of the sack of Rome, which the two partners sought recourse in building—so to speak—their formal universe: a throne-chair, a Venus-Hotentot used as the base for a console, a window display reminiscent of the 'fillettes'[1] of Louis XI or a Menhir mirror for a man's vanity. It was thus with considerable resolve that Garouste and Bonetti made a clean sweep of the leading principles of the decorative arts of the twentieth century, whose watchword had long been that "ornamentation was a crime", distancing themselves at the same time from the elegant and very French 'art de vivre' refined to such an extent as to become, through English grace and the blood of a revolution, a pregnant model of civilization. It was in fact to nothing short of a re-founding of the decorative arts, far from theoretical dictates and other proponents of good taste that Garouste and Bonetti invite us—summoning us to a place where the charms of the strange and of the magical mix with the unheard-of luxury of simplicity.

Elsewhere, this critique of modernism and its avatars was more orthodox, focusing all the while on modernism as something that had not been—or could not be—gone beyond. From Italian radical design, from which stemmed the Alchimia and Memphis movements, or the 'post-modernism' of someone like Venturi, the various forms of questioning were always defined by an ideological and globalizing point of view. Garouste and Bonetti, on

[1] Small torture cages. *Translator's note*

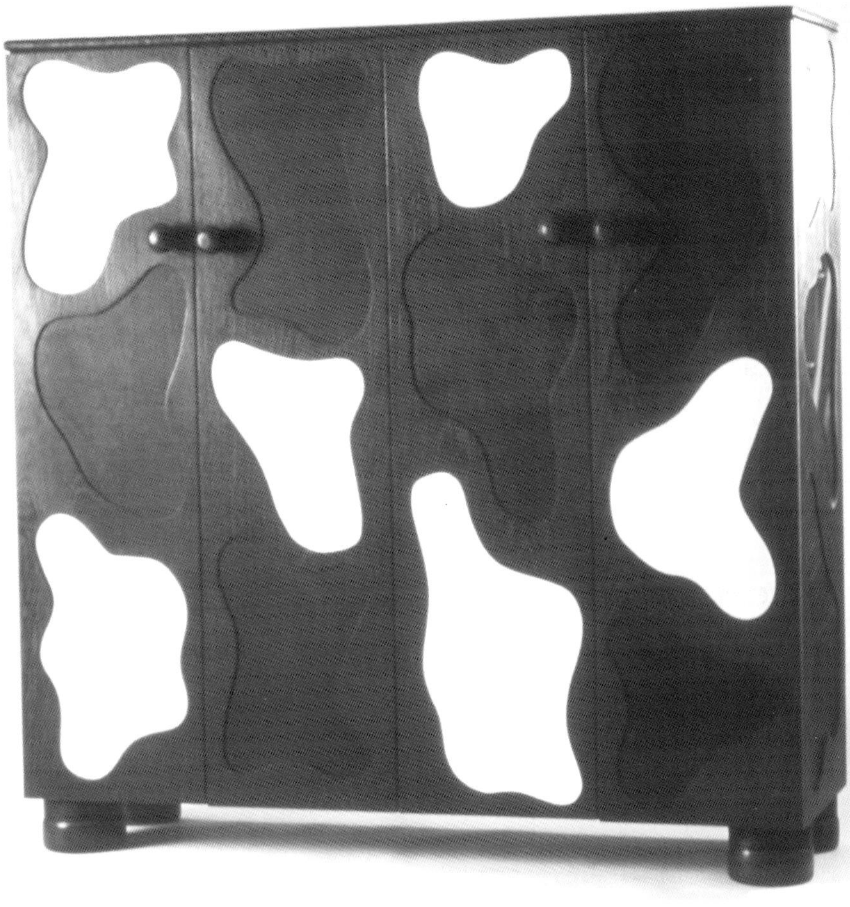

Atoll cupboard, 1994
wengé, leather and mirror, 131x130x40 cm
Ed. Neotu (Paris)
Phot. : Neotu.

the contrary, taking full advantage of the 'libertarian gaps' of these theories, steer clear of theory but rely instead upon subjective points of view: those of taste and of the local in their reinvention of an eternal history.

Delectare cernentes Where stringent modernism had evacuated the body of desire and its fluctuating, circumstance-specific positioning, in favor of a hygienic, rational body that was unequivocal in its attitudes, the neo-Baroque movement of the 1980s—of which Garouste and Bonetti were such magnificent representatives—claims on the other hand to dazzle, to grasp the mind from all sides in such a way as to exacerbate the affects, blazing a trail for jubilation in order to better free the yokes of thought. Beauty is thus triumphant, and nothing is able to stand in its way; any analysis is relegated to an approximation of pleasure, a last-ditch solution, a useless attempt at eluding its fascination. At the risk of loss of self, we abandon ourselves to the exaltation of the senses without trying to master them. Surrounded by beauty—a concept that the twentieth century has been very determined to render fuzzy and non-operational in many areas, that the history of the humanities has taught us to relativize to such an extent as to neutralize it—we fictionalize our environment and ourselves. From a speculative position—that of modernity—where hypotheses have always had to be measured against the yardstick of totalitarianism, we thrust ourselves into specularity where intended meaning dissolves and diffracts into a happy drive, free once again to smash slogans and rules of proper conduct and political correctness as well as taste. "Constructing sense is nothing by deconstructing meaning”, as Jean-François Lyotard was able to proclaim in *Discours, Figure.* This mutism on the part of beauty, because it paradoxically engendered meaning, albeit only that of its own disappearance, has been pointed out both by Roland Barthes (“beauty shall be mute, abandoned to itself, deprived of any previously existing code”, [SZ]) and Michel de Certeau (“the annulment of a spoken discursivity, the proliferation of meaning backsliding toward its point of silence”, *La Fable mystique*); in practical terms, both authors invite the reader to set aside his knowledge—literary in the one case, religious in the other—to better gain access. In a different mode, this is also what Sollers (“experience ourselves, whatever the cost may be, as fiction”, *Logiques*) and Lyotard (“like the dream, the pictorial object is thought of in keeping with the function of hallucinatory representation and of illusion”, *Des dispositifs pulsionnels*) are after, in inviting us to let an unconscious knowledge to “well up” within us. Garouste and Bonetti were amongst the first of their generation —no doubt because one began a career as a visual artist and the other has accompanied one over the course of many years—to turn these lessons to good account, taking advantage of the conclusions of the ineffable when others were still trying to create a ‘vocabulary’. Converting the show rooms of the Christian Lacroix fashion house provided a brilliant demonstration: respecting—even emphasizing—the personality of their patron, the two creators set up a total space exalting a world of sensations where the swishes of the colorful silks of fashion shows mixed with the always somewhat silly wonderment of female fashion editors, the legend of Haute Couture, caught between the unabashed privileges of his customers and the vanities of their suppliers, with the tracery

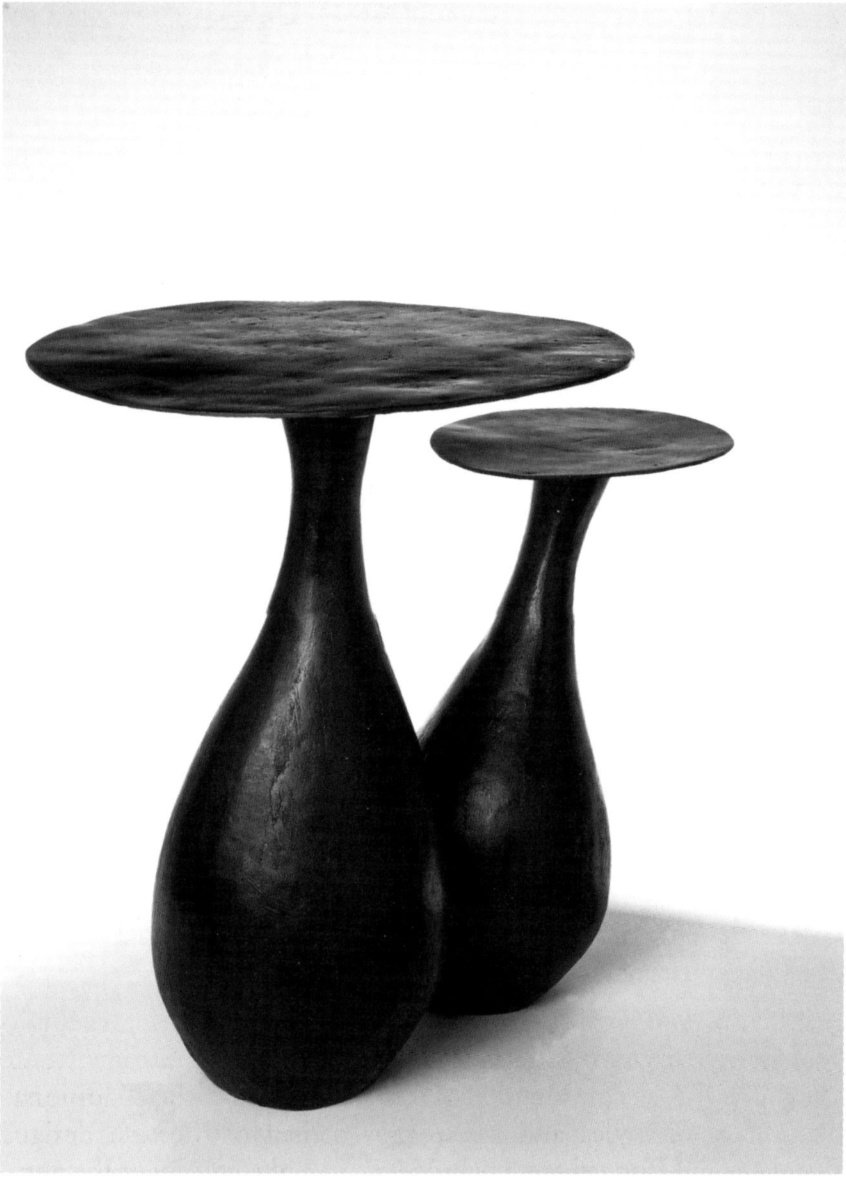

You and Me, 1994
double gueridon
patinated bronze
Ed. David Gill Gallery (London)

of a partition, the patina of a wall, the violence of a shocking pink or the excessive size of a seat.

They were subsequently able to reiterate the success of this encirclement on a number of private work-sites: in Hong Kong, working marvels with chinoiseries, or on Hydra, exalting the Mediterranean, demonstrating the same sureness of hand as they had in the case of Christian Lacroix. In the hypertrophy of signs of reference or, on the contrary, in their very symbolic rarefaction, Garouste and Bonetti have constantly made visible the state of the world—without ever imposing a world of their own penchant, like a decorator might.

Exhibitio It is as playwrights of the passions that the two creators have exhibited the world, well deserving the somewhat forged term of 'Baroque' that the press has so often pinned on them. "All terrestrial beings are assembled and exalted, before being delivered to their end" (Walter Benjamin, *The Origin of German Tragic Drama*). In the theater of the world, through systematic recourse to charms and ornaments, wherever they may come from, Garouste and Bonetti have been able, in Vladimir Jankelevitch's words (in *Le je ne sais quoi et le presque rien*), "to capture occurrences, occasions and manners".

The designer duo claims to restitute all their aesthetic experiences, all their historical references, all their intelligence of situations in a continuous stream. Giving up the traditional hierarchies of styles and the ethnocentrism of Western design, Garouste and Bonetti are working within a philosophy of the non-discreet, of the see-all and show-all, in a perpetual reworking of codes, the permanent displacement of limits and the examination of an open field of virtualities. As if it were always necessary to expand integration still further, the culture of the two creators is one of totality, impossible not by default or by accident, but because it always leads into an endless navigation where standards—between excess and perfect decoding—are merely the often trivial figure of a hidden order.

Garouste and Bonetti's prodigiousness, however, their culture of the outrageous—somewhat in the manner of English eccentrics—at times displaying its excessiveness and deploying its ostentation, does tend to bring into play, as Christine Buci-Glucksmann has pointed out in *La Folie du Voir* dealing with the Baroque aesthetics, sadness and its pleasures, illusions combined and reinforced with great pomp, "the work of cultural mourning", to which the great representatives of the Baroque lead us. This annihilation produced by the strategy of the "power to see all" is exactly in keeping with that of the functioning of anamorphoses, balancing between the deployment of form and the necessity of a point of view where inscription is visible.

From jubilation to mortification: such is the Baroque path of which old Europe chose, in the course of the twentieth century, to shed all but the deathly remains. From the Wiener Werkstatte to the Viennese body-art of the 1970s, Austria was the most perfect example, while old England, drugged up and tripped out on the young American nation, invented a more charming and worldly figure. From the Omega group to Oliver Messel via Edith Wharton or Cecil Beaton, it has been in the realm of parties and shows that the spirit of the Baroque has best been illustrated in

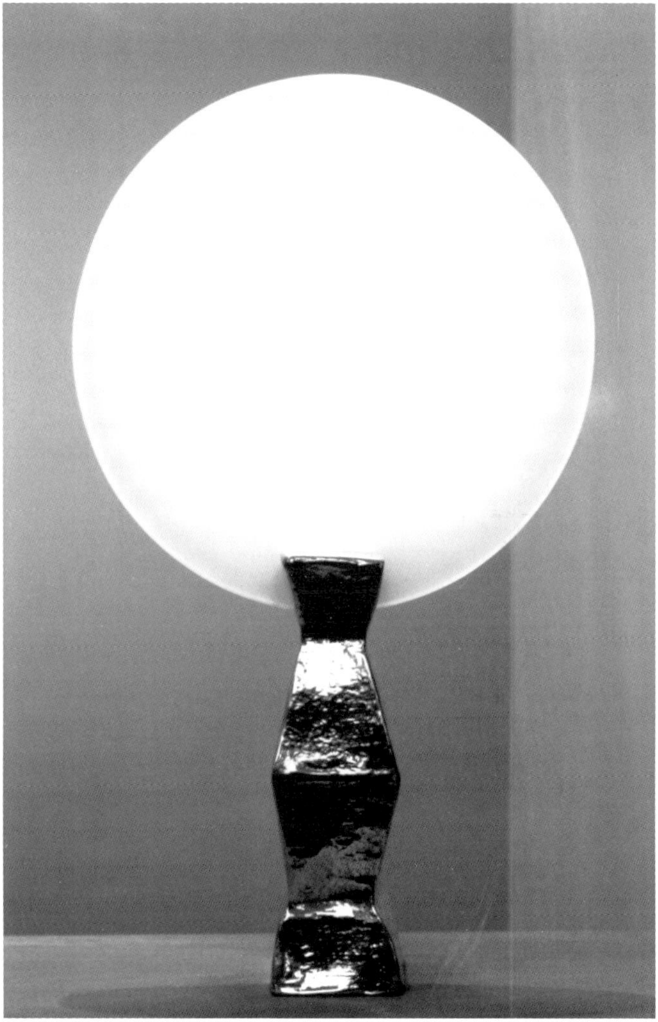

Lune lamp, 1984
bronze and frosted glass, 40 cm
Ed. En attendant les barbares (Paris)
Phot. : Simon Kentish

twentieth-century England, more recently rebounding in the domain of contemporary art (Damien Hirst or the Chapman brothers for instance) or of communication (the trials and tribulations of the Royals, up to and including the use being made today of Princess Diana's death.

In France, Garouste and Bonetti—after Christian Bérard or Emilio Terry in the 1940s and Philippe Jullian in the two decades which followed—are the sole true representatives (confirmed by their success in England) of this tradition, made up of the jubilation of the 'madness to see' and of an exiled exasperation on the social scene which succeeds in "avoiding the boredom which many experience in relation to the modern text, film or avant-garde painting: boredom means that one cannot produce the text—cannot play it, undo it, make it go" (Roland Barthes, *Revue d'Esthétique*, n°3). It is to this starting point that Garouste and Bonetti's prolific production beckons us.

Tratatto delle acutezze To do so, the two creators have brought to bear—and it is this which has always attracted adhesion to their work in spite of its often being pigeonholed and having fingers pointed at it—an *esprit de finesse*, a 'concetto' which, in the history of forms, is more closely related to the literature of Gongora or Gracian, or more recently of Le Clezio or Almira.

In 1639, Peregrini, in his *Tratatto delle acutezze* defined its component parts as including the marvelous, the ambiguous, the aberrant, obscure metaphor, allusion, ingeniousness and sophism. Garouste and Bonetti integrated them into their own aspirations, perpetually oscillating between the precision of the decorative (even when it cannot keep up with the excess load) and the evidence of the project (even when it practically illustrates a perverse complacency with regard to the sponsor).

Their furniture production is punctuated, first of all, by the marvelous—that Elizabeth Garouste in particular claims to represent—which has evidently come to materialize the environment of such and such a princess, like the *Sweet Dreams* bed with bronze branches which produce golden fruit or the *Petit Nuage* side-table where the rock-crystal tray is studded with cabochons of amethyst. From nature transfigured by its imitation (bronze as a tree branch) or by its use (rock crystal as a metaphor of a cloud) there is born a wondrousness, even imbricated in what amounts to a very classical image of luxury, whose authenticity lies not in the improbability of acts habitually associated with it, but rather in the entirely material veracity of Garouste and Bonetti's decor. If some of their creations are clearly situated on only one side of the world—that of opulence—most of them nonetheless illustrate perfectly this ambiguity in which their charms are nestled. The coarseness of the raw terracotta slabs, the rusted or blackened sheet metal, stands in opposition to the sophistication of the whole in the small *Collerette* cabinet. An ostentation that some would qualify as showy, as some learned pipe dream of India as seen by Venice in the cream-colored lacquer and gilded bronze *India* pedestal table. A powerful—even violent—decorative effect and the feeble use value of the *Barbaric* chair whose weight makes it exceedingly cumbersome; or, on the contrary, functionalism versus formal effect, in the ashtray or the carafe for Ricard. One could go on infinitely listing the ambiguities, indeterminacies and absences of 'parti pris' with which Garouste and Bonetti amuse themselves.

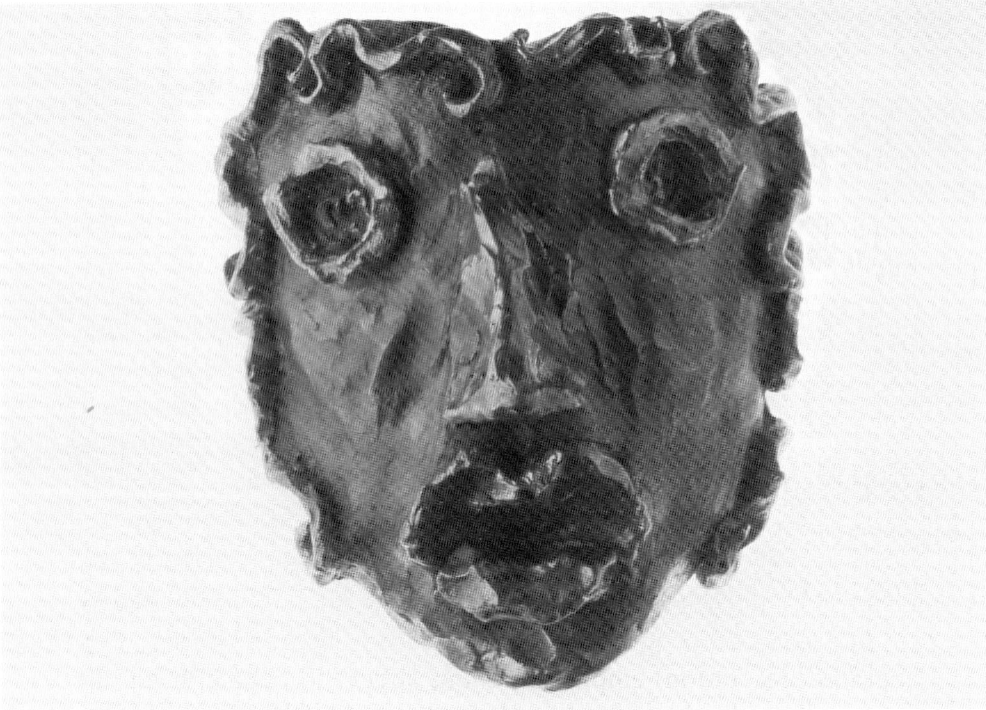

Masque wall-lamp, 1984
bronze, 26x23x10 cm
B.G.H Ed. (Paris)
Phot. : Studio Harry Bréjat

Beyond that lies the question of taste, not so much in terms of respect for fixed canons and referential images as in the thoroughly contemporary elaboration of new standards able to take both recognition and provocation into account. Elsewhere, it is the aberrant which comes to the fore, as in the *Prince Impérial* chair, conceived in the minds of its creators as the improbable field chair of the son of a French emperor from a very real colonial war; or the swelling shape of the *Palerme* chest-of-drawers, bulging to the point of perverting the genre of reference (the chest-of-drawers known as 'tombeau'). But the power of such aberrations staged by Garouste and Bonetti lies not only in their sources of inspiration or the 'stories' their objects tell; it also stems from a certain technical immaturity, related above all to the connection between the materials, forcing the creators into veritable acrobatics of fabrication (as in the pivoting lamps, with disproportionate arms) and the stubbornness in relation to the initial idea (pieces of Venetian furniture enhanced with engraved decoration) employing a *laca povera* technique, taken up once again in the *Agriente* chest through the use of photocopies).

From an aberrant imagination to which nothing can stand up, to aberrations stemming from the resistance of the real, Garouste and Bonetti insist on the theatrical nature of their work: 'trompe l'œil', a concentrate of contradictory forms of know-how, the heterogeneity of feelings, active forces and resistances are at work in order to produce in spite of everything the physical objects which are so undeniably present. With the *Turtle* ashtray, it is not only the angel of the bizarre which came to animate the work of Garouste and Bonetti, but also that particular type of metaphor referred to as 'obscure' because the elements it sets in place are not obvious, and bear no evidence of the object itself and its function—the type of metaphor which designers are generally most fond of. Nothing of the sort here: how could a dice, a string of pearls, a bandanna, a pair of lace panties, a pair of Adidas and a shade of porcelain have any rapport—even metaphorical—with the ashtray? Garouste and Bonetti's discourse is entirely different: it represents a contemporary vision of femininity, expressing all the ambiguities of the changing place of women in today's society, at once forced to make themselves up (the shade of porcelain) and to run for herself (the sports shoes), to rely on their sexuality (the panties) as well as on luck (the dice)—all of which contributes to making a metaphor out of an addiction to tobacco. It is this distance, this deformation in the connection which makes the metaphor obscure, steering it away from an overly direct vision and transforming any idea of decor into a veritable iconological key. One comes across this same phenomenon in many of the two creators' objects, no doubt because the motif is more difficult to turn back onto a piece of furniture. Such is the case of the *Pandora* jewel box made of broken mirrors (the melancholy of finery), the *Masque* wall-light for Christian Lacroix —the nose of which is an endless screw (the philosophy of dressmaking)—and the mechanical decor of *Étranges végétations* (identification of taste) or the applications of the *Boogie Woogie* vases (inscribing it, nonetheless, in modernism). In this regard, decor is obviously never a surcharge, not even an ornamental motif, but is always at the service of this power of representation which the object or the piece of furniture has in relation to the act. It can take the figure of the enigma, of an obscure metaphor, referring back to a hidden, occasionally esoteric, meaning.

For the furniture, it is allusion which often takes primacy over the metaphorical dimension, at times in an obvious way—as for

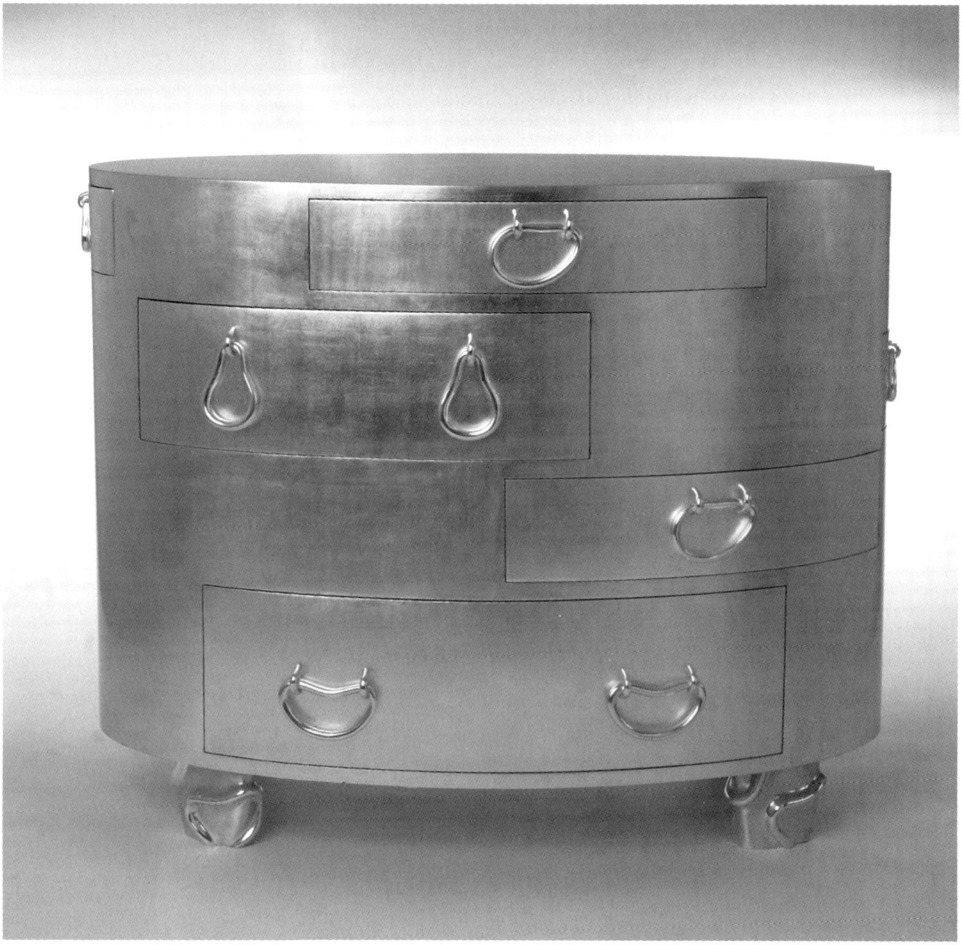

Kawakubo, 1994
oval chest of drawers
wood, gilded with a white gold leaf, silver plated bronze, 123x100x55 cm
Ed. David Gill Gallery (London)

instance in the way Garouste and Bonetti dealt with a commission on the tiger theme, sometimes in a more hidden way as in the *Kawakubo* silver chest-of-drawers whose rich white-gold leafing undoes the minimalism which is the trademark of the designer of Comme des Garçons. In the same way, the Sèvres cabinet carries out a double staging: both of Hokusai's famous wave and the Manufacture de Sèvres' 'fin de siècle' infatuation for Japanese things. Not to mention the countless references to art (arte povera associated with the *Rocher* table, the Matissian foliage in the *Rohan* day-bed, Jean Royère's use of raffia, the Neapolitan coral work associated with the jewels for Best Friend, the Bracelli constructions with the *Oriflamme* floor-lamp, and so on) scattered throughout Garouste and Bonetti's work. Sometimes the allusions are more personal and can actually stand as a rebus, especially when the duo creates whole sets of objects. At that stage, signs cease to have a conventional character but become willfully hieroglyphic. There again the motif escapes its ornamental status and becomes language. At that point, the keys of scholarly culture or of familiarity (private jokes) are required to decode the meaning, and confer all the meaning to the possession of the object.

The ingeniousness in Garouste and Bonetti's work lies in their transforming of motif into structure. In the work they did for the "Trapani" collection, for instance, the branch of coral—whose use as a motif has been attested to since antiquity—becomes the very structure of a pedestal table or of a fruit cup; for the piece of furniture known as *Bobine*, the ten-centimeter strip, so relished by Buren, becomes the emergence of form; in the eleven-legged table, the tracery of the wrought-iron legs itself draws the tray's support; the disk-like form of the Ricard bottle allows it to be stored easily on the shelf. Thus, generally speaking, Garouste and Bonetti provide extremely simple answers to technical problems; with what could appear attractive naïveté, they discover obvious, sometimes primitive solutions where others would practically have resorted to the calculations of engineers.

Garouste and Bonetti's system therefore is logical, in appearance at any rate, taking up the ingredients of storytellers and iconographers, combining the impulses of poets and 'tinkerers', exalting the lively and the melancholic; but it is a hot logic where some item always crops up and troubles any attempt at generalization. Beyond the result of this hybridization process of different logics, there is a veritable resistance to theory which without any doubt whatsoever encloses the two creators in a world of recipes even as they devote themselves incessantly to newness and surprise.

La Cuisine-objet for the Guggenheim, a noteworthy project done within the framework of the French art exhibition organized in New York by the Pompidou Center, and which never came out in its initial form, is a perfect illustration of Garouste and Bonetti's 'concetto'. Bringing together earlier characteristics with matchless panache, the work is no longer merely a piece of furniture or object but an entire kitchen: stove, sink, larder, pots, tea-towels, and so on, the whole thing completely gilded with gold leaf. A kitchen from the seedier side of Dickens' London, transfigured by the touch of a magic and golden wand by some *Alice in Wonder land*, the aberrant representation of one of the key elements of functionality in the house, obscurely representing both the French tradition—the large kitchen, the gilding evoking the splendors of Versailles, the excesses of reason—but also the very functioning of

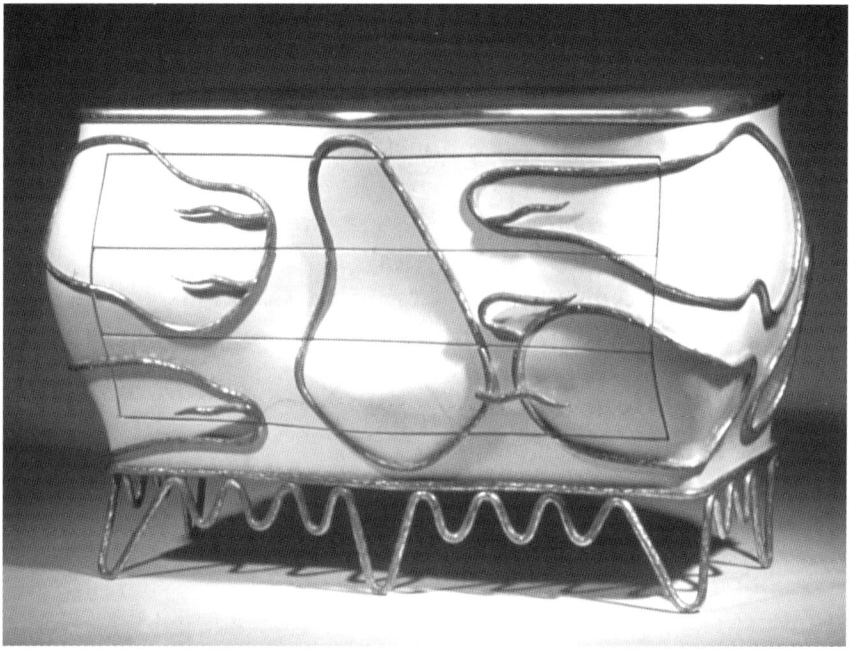

Palerme, chest of drawers, 1992
lacquered wood, gilded wrought iron, 105x153x75 cm
Ed. Neotu (Paris)
Phot: Karin Knoblich

institutions dissimulating their misery, their everydayness beneath the extraordinary, evoking the work of fixation and derision, the fantasy pop of Jeff Koons or Damien Hirst, ingeniously faithful to their creations without actually being a veritable piece of furniture. And in fact the computer-generated image shown at the exhibition instead and in place of the piece itself had to suffice all on its own.

Here again, Garouste and Bonetti are working along the lines of Federico Zuccari's *disegno fantastico-artificiale* (*L'idea de' pittori, scultori ed architetti*, 1607)—in other words, constructions of the strange and curious, 'caprices' and 'follies', 'factories' and 'fantasies', grotesques and 'forgeries'; an anti-naturalist production which nevertheless draws an artificial image from the imitation of nature, whether it be in creating "theater scenes, fountains, loggia, gardens, rooms, temples, palaces, machines, clocks, chimeras" or *La Cuisine* for the Guggenheim.

Ut picturia poesis... One is therefore obliged to think of nature, in Garouste and Bonetti's work, as a complex of feelings and not as a model of reference, a state. It is a part of human nature which the two use to construct a narrative, centered around the user or client who commissioned the work, who is then imagined—fantasized about—in his emotional and social life. It is the impulse of narration, much more than the impulse of style, which guides Garouste and Bonetti—as is testified to by their moving on from the neo-barbarism of their beginnings to the flamboyant Baroque which established their glory, then further on to the well-tempered modernism which is today their passport to the industrial world. A branch is still a branch, or rather the image of a branch is still the image of a branch, be it made of wood, wrought iron, bronze or plastic. It is its context, like the word in the language or the sentence in the story which confers its meaning: seduction of the primitive in the case of some museum curator, pantheism in the case of some cosmopolitan woman client seeking to root her own culture in a welcoming land, the romanticism of the young couple who were offered a bed made of bronze branches for their wedding night or more prosaically, an ersatz green plant for the huge tree of gilded wrought iron bearing electric fruit in the overexposed living room of a lawyer.

Where infinite style links the past and the future, justifying all the old forms—even at the price of decontextualizing them—and all the anticipations (it suffices to call to mind the various representations of which it was the object at the dawn of the twentieth century), narration on the other hand runs to its own end, to its deadlock, to closure and completion. Practically all of Garouste and Bonetti's work is along these lines: each step is a story usually told right to the end, and to which they rarely have occasion to return, only when the conclusion has not been drawn, as for instance with the piece of *Bobine* furniture or the series for Lafuma, which has in fact reached its logical conclusion today with the furniture designed for the 3 Suisses mail-order retailer. In this way, one series of fictions follows upon another, the two designers summoning our adhesion to one after the other: that of neo-primitivism, breaking with design and classical decoration right up until 1986; that of 'glamour' until 1992, bound up with the great sexual fantasmatics, so plenteous as the end of the century approaches; that of the necessary rereading of modernism once the bipolar ideologies were definitively out of the way, taking a stab at the luxury of formal rigor as well as a subsequent possible return to biomorphism. But it is always as near as possible to life, and not on the

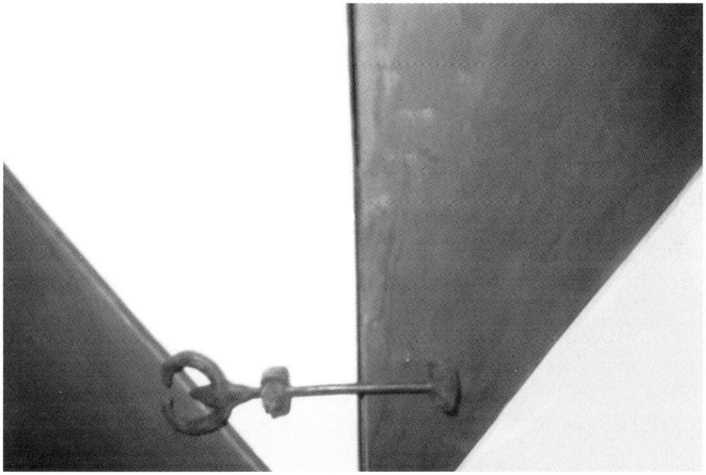

Cabinet 90, 1990
detail of the fastener
oxydized wrought iron, bicolored terracottas
Ed. Neotu (Paris)
Phot: Neotu

material with regard to their objectives, notably in the creation of the *Barbaric* chair in 1981.

It would doubtless be more exact to make reference to Jean Royère, on whom today there regrettably exists no study whatsoever (despite the impressive archives held at the Museum of Decorative Arts in Paris). Thus, Royère's extremely prolific work remains little known, subject practically speaking to the availability of pieces—many of which can unfortunately no longer be located on the market, in particular the deliveries Royère made in Egypt, Lebanon and Iran. The same heterogeneity is at work in Royère's production as in that of Garouste and Bonetti who do not hesitate to borrow from the register of the collusions, unexpected confrontations and original hybridizations which are so characteristic of surrealism. There is a cultivated—and in that respect very domesticated—heterogeneity which reaches the unbearable in Royère's as well as Garouste and Bonetti's work: from having been incongruous, the complicity between two terms quickly becomes doxy. Like Royère, Garouste and Bonetti are as prolific in their recourse to the oniric as to the 'conventional': while Royère makes star-shaped marquetry out of straw for a bedroom design, Garouste and Bonetti produce obsessional daisies; Royère makes an austere nesting of straw and pots and pans (like something out of Hop o' My Thumb), while Garouste and Bonetti come up with a double mirror depicting a narcissus; or take Royère's polar-bear sofa as opposed to the pair's *Koala* daybed, Royère's pseudo-Dutch chandelier, versus their 'rotunda' tables with sculpted tracery. Neither Royère nor Garouste and Bonetti seek technical prowess: when it does occur—which is relatively rare—it is there as something natural and deduced, rather than summoned and

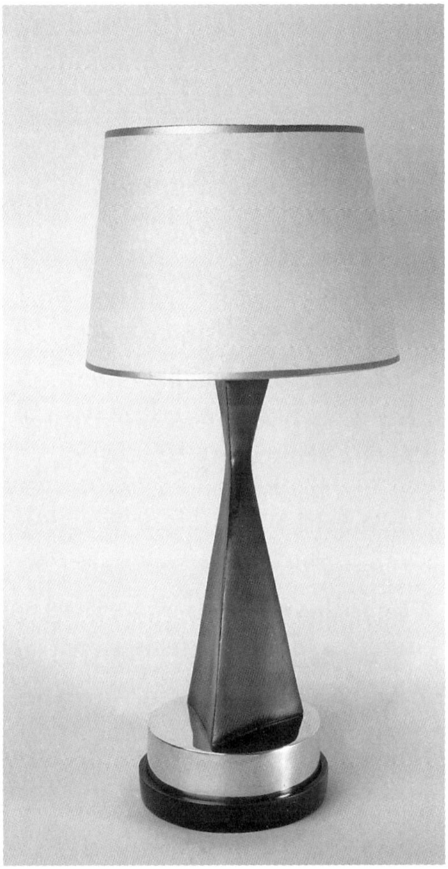

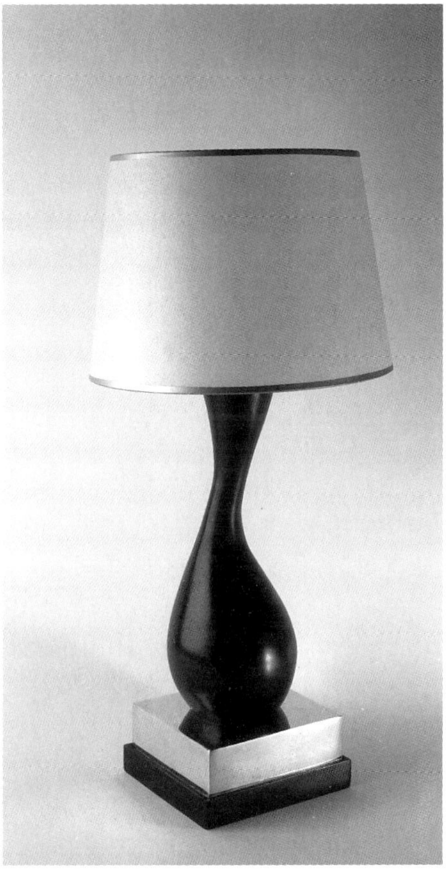

The Fake pair, lamps, 1996
patinated bronze and gilded polished bronze
Frederic de Luca Gallery (Paris)
Phot. : Denis Menou

demonstrative. Both are very much part of the very French *esprit* of successfully combining grandiloquence with derision, contradiction with logic, and culture with the simplicity of references.

Yet Bonetti, an Italian Swiss, and Garouste, fond of mentioning her Russian grandmothers, have been able to sink their roots in elsewhere, in particular in the Italy of Gio Ponti on whom Ugo La Pietra has written a noteworthy book published in 1995 by Rizzoli—the following passage of which, taken from the introduction, fits our two creators like a glove: "The difficulty that official criticism encounters in its reading of Gio Ponti may stem from its instinct to work incessantly along a line of compromise between rationalist codes and a certain attention to tradition, classical ideas, marginal forms of expression and the use of decoration. These lines of compromise have always disoriented critics and reinforced Gio Ponti's image. Ponti was not always appreciated by his contemporaries, no doubt because of his success. Whatever his success, however, it never swayed him from his attachment to his most happily ingenuous fantasies, from his joyous and inspired tone, his almost infantile curiosity and his pleasure in conceiving and imagining things; and he never sacrificed his values, unlike most of those who, like him, attained power and recognition."

Of course Garouste and Bonetti have not yet had either the longevity or the diversity of experiences (architecture, furniture design, industrial design, interior decorating, publishing activities, painting, teaching, talent-scouting) of Gio Ponti, active over the course of a half-century. Yet they share with him a prolific character and a predilection for mixtures of the most classical material with the most adventurous, the richest with the most ponderously trivial.

But above all, the absence of any overly cumbersome theorizing: "I want to make house-houses (and not 'organic' or 'rational' houses, or of whatever other label), I want to make bed-beds and cupboard-cupboards.... I believe that a piece of furniture, though always functional, must engage the imagination of the designer as much as that of whoever looks at it."

Garouste and Bonetti, like Gio Ponti, start on the basis of both formal rigor (that of the classical age) and social utopia (that of modernism), even if these are sometimes concealed by a hypertrophied expressiveness and an undeniable decorative exuberance. A free and continuous flow of creativity, intuitive potential, ideology of spontaneity: such are the ingredients of what amounts to a cultural attitude with regard to modernity, conceived of by Ponti and Garouste and Bonetti as a historical continuity, the consequence of the history of forms, and not as an ideological rupture with the nineteenth century. Which is why Ponti's like Garouste and Bonetti's reading of modern design or decorative arts—which some might judge to be a little naïve—is not accompanied by either a recurrent and 'formatted' approach, or any sense of guilt with regard to the idea of luxury. In spite of appearances, both Ponti and Garouste and Bonetti are also very much at ease with notions of 'popular culture' and industrial production—and it is in these domains that Gio Ponti has accomplished some of his most significant production, such as the *Supperleggera* chair for Cassina.

It is even thanks to this uncomplexed affluence that Garouste and Bonetti, like Royère or Ponti, fall outside the category of kitsch in which they have at times been pigeonholed. If kitsch functionalizes a need for beauty and pleasure, it does so by

man, benefiting from his belonging to both western and far-eastern culture, or of the inexpensive, composable world of a young French couple, sending away for mail-order merchandise.

Thus the world of Garouste and Bonetti is not one of gentle and inspired dreamers, inveterate nature-lovers or old-fashioned minds with delusions of grandeur; nor is it primitive or Baroque, elegant or fashionable, classical or far-fetched. The world of Garouste and Bonetti is our world—our world of the end of the twentieth century, shot through with contradictions of social necessity such as the power of money, the pleasures of communication and the need for a new retreat, for seduction as well as intelligence.

It is often the world of the rich, whether through old money or new, and the powerful who need that dose of insolence mixed with culture that the two designers provide. It is also the world of a middle class steeped in nostalgia who see in Garouste and Bonetti an acceptable model of modernity. It will also be—if the two creators manage to develop an industrial activity that began with the lines for Ricci and the Montpellier tramway—one of banal and daily consumption of beauty.

In another, far lighter register—though not altogether without a bite of irony—it is the linking of objects and decor to ways of life, to actions and their implication which Philippe Jullian illustrated so masterfully in *Les Styles* (Plon, 1961)—a book which doubtless represented for Garouste and Bonetti, making the most out of his considerable erudition, a veritable little bible, a mine of humorous notations and a formidable reserve of lucidity.

Fiat Lux

Nadia Croquet (N.): Élizabeth, could you say something about your relationship with objects before you met Mattia?

Élizabeth Garouste (E.): My childhood was a determinate factor in that regard. I come from an immigrant family whose goal was, more or less, to find a place for itself in the 'bourgeois' world in France. My parents had no money and no inheritance. They tried to create a world made up above all of the fairly diverse collection of stuff my father picked up at flea markets. In my bed, I was always curled up because I was absolutely convinced that everything moved at night. I was afraid of objects. I was really traumatized, to such an extent that I practically wanted to commit suicide—but I wasn't brave enough to. It took me years to get away from that sort of pantheism. I spent a large portion of my youth with my father doing purchasing at the Aligre Market because his store was close by and, at the time, it was a pretty fantastic kind of place. Although it became very fashionable after the 1970s, at the time nobody liked the place and it ended up influencing a great deal. Everyday my father brought home different *objets d'art.* At the market, there were jumbles of things but people were more interested in the pots and pans than the paintings. My grandmothers who came from the outback of Russia told about how they lived in *isbas.* I lived in a mixture of different realms of imagery, like in a dream. And then I had the good fortune to go to a school which was quite open and had a good artistic level: the École Alsacienne in Paris where we had true artists as teachers, painters who let us work in a very open and very free spirit. I mean, before we could even draw very well, they instilled a sort of freedom in us. We worked on graffiti and Matisse-style lines and we just went wild with colors. For a very introverted young girl like myself, it really helped me to loosen up. I was lucky to have parents who registered me and my brother in the Decorative Arts studio for under-fifteen year olds. My father, who was always building things although he worked in a different trade altogether, regularly took us to the museum. I was oriented toward a mystico-invented world: all inanimate objects had a soul. I would speak to a sideboard, or to my bed; I would do ceremonials one after the other and each thing represented was like a totem. I was always attracted to the very theatrical world of furniture, like something out of *Alice in Wonderland*: terrifying objects, some merely dreamt. I began my studies in that direction because I did a year at the preparatory studio of the Académie Charpentier. Then I entered the École Camondo where I stayed only two of the requisite five years. That was at about the time of the events of May 1968; I must have been nineteen years old and the entire straightjacket was just blown off the system. That instilled the desire to create and the need to move closer to the idea of desire. Unfortunately, my private life was such that I was unable to start right off in the furniture field so I worked in my parents' shop: a Tilbury fashion-shoe shop—which began to drive me a bit nuts. My friends would all come to see me on Saturday nights, and I had the feeling I was in an aquarium. So as not to be a prisoner of this environment, I wrote criticism of children's books on the side and wrote a play for children with a girlfriend. Meanwhile, I married Gerard who was very open and very involved in painting and the theater. Instead of leaving school with a certain state of mind, I was very open-minded about art and kept very diverse company. I also took part in costume-making, and set-design with you, Nadia, do you remember? It really was a fractured environment where, at the time, people had time and money wasn't everything; there was no strategic careerism going on. Life carried us along.

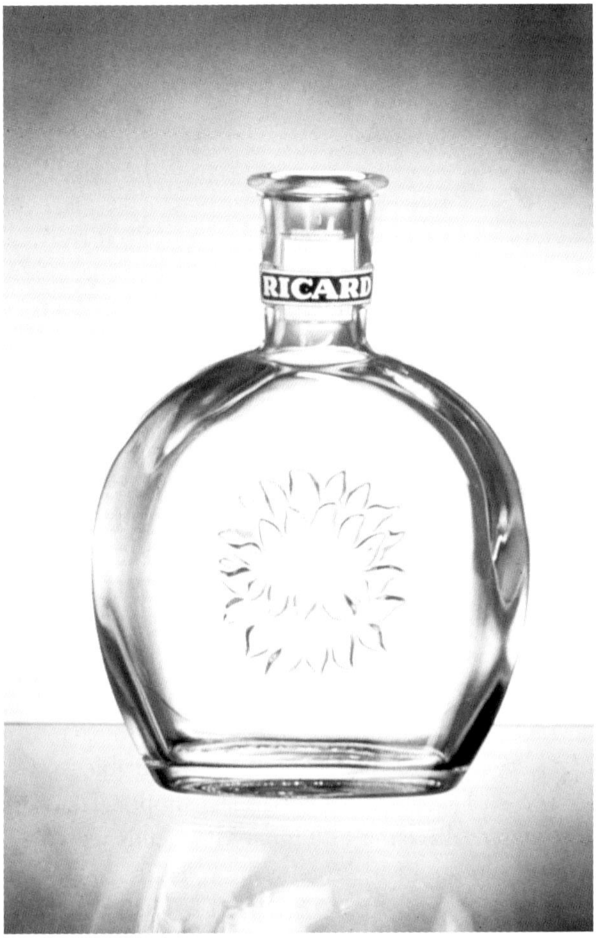

Ricard carafe, 1994 (18 cm)
Agent: Kréo
Phot: Frédéric Moulin

Laurent Le Bon (L): To come back to the École Alsacienne where you said you benefited from high-quality teaching, do you think education is very influential in the appreciation of artworks, in particular of your creations?

E: Artistic education really is something that is truly lacking in France. It's true in every field, even at the level of people running businesses, and it has consequences: even if you have a clothing or furniture or door-handle factory, an artistic education lets you see things in a different way. For children, that is of capital importance. Its absence is a serious shortcoming.

L: Have you tried to give your two sons an artistic education?

E: Well, I haven't attempted to teach them art in a school-like way, but of course they would come to the theater, they would come with us to see certain films, and above all they would see us working in our studios. They went to see exhibitions with Gerard. They took part as well in a certain cultural life. The whole adventure we embarked upon at La Source in Normandy came from that same concern with artistic education: the idea was to use artistic practices for the social reintegration of children from a rural setting. My dream is to work on designing a teaching building.

N: I recall a whole circle including Philippe Starck, Adeline André.... Today it seems extraordinary to think that all those people who were the same age all lived together. But at the time, nobody was known. In the house in Bourg-la-Reine, where Elizabeth and Gerard lived, there were a lot of people from different walks of life—theater, photography, design, fashion—who all came together around the meals Elizabeth had cooked. She's an excellent cook by the way.

L: The first objects were born at that time?

E: No, not at all.

N: First there was the arrival of Mattia, who was a catalyst.

E: I was the one who had to keep the household going: that's why I worked for about eight years with my parents. Until the day Gerard began earning a living at The Palace and The Privilege where he had been taken on to do all the stage set-designs. So he said to me: "Now I can get by. You can stop, if you want." Between times, I had done a bit of work with Mattia because I had asked him to redo the decor of the store and to do the window displays. Adeline André had done a collection of clothes and shoes—that was in 1979. At the birth of my second son, I quit the job and a new life began. For the lighting design of the new club, Le Privilège, all our friends came over and everyone made a mask in our little garden. Mattia stayed on a bit longer. He was trying to figure out what to do with himself: why not make furniture together? That's how it all started.

N: How had you met Mattia?

E: Mattia was initially a friend of my brother's, David Rochline. He had acted in one of David's plays, *A toutes les gloires de France*. He was living with a very trendy woman, a clothing designer. It was a whole crowd: they were sort of feeling their way along. After The Privilege had achieved some success, Gerard basically took off and had an exhibition of his paintings: it worked out, so he just sort of abandoned us all.

L: During the much-described Palace period, you attended parties, entirely ephemeral creations, you made up the container so to speak as well as being part of the contents. Did you go out every evening during these magic moments?

E: I didn't so much want to as had to. There were some really pretty exceptional parties and very often our alarm clock would ring at one o'clock in the morning and we'd go to the Palace at around two o'clock until eight o'clock.

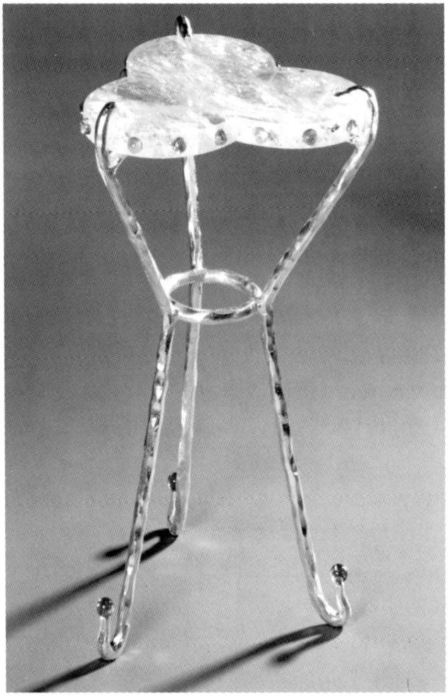

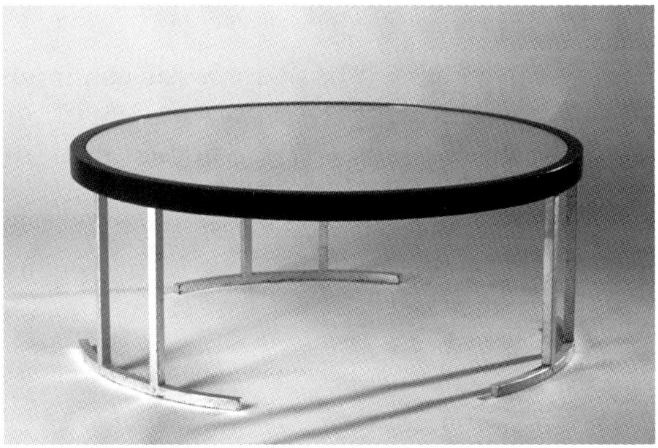

Petit Nuage, side-table, 1991
rock crystal, amethyst, silver-plated wrought iron
Ed. Eva-Maria Melchers (Bremen, Germany)
Phot.: Studio Seehamp, Bremen

Ring, coffee table, 1994.
mirror, wengé wood, gilded metal, 40x101 cm
Ed. Neotu (Paris)
Phot: Neotu

L: How did you initially deal with your environment being inhabited by evening visitors? Did you think that it was going to be a mythical success or did you think of it in a bit more ephemeral fashion?

E: I realize that right from the beginning I liked the idea of illusion. Our actions were not governed by any strategy. Everything is usually based on impulse. It was the idea of true and false and of making things theatrical. People go to nightclubs to be seen, so we offered them a theater decor made under the same conditions. Actually, it received very little coverage in the magazines. People went past an enormous, Renaissance-inspired porch and then down a staircase—they were sort of conditioned for what was to come. There was a podium, then the room with the plaster net curtains, pilasters, painted canvases, chairs with frescos and large wall-hangings. With very few elements, the idea was to create a general atmosphere. Le Privilège was a club within a club. The site was classed as protected, everything had to be able to be taken apart.

N: And the masks?

E: The mask—whether it be figurative or not, inspired from museums of primitive art, from the film *Beauty and the Beast* —remained a going concern throughout those years. The first mask in bronze was done in Marocco for "En attendant les Barbares". Later, the nose, twisted like Pinocchio's when he tells a lie, lit up the Christian Lacroix showrooms. There is another one actually, right in our publishing house, "BGH", which has a wilder look. For our next exhibition in the David Gill Gallery, there is going to be an emperor with an elephant's nose. Many themes, including the figure, nature and so on, crop up recurrently in our work over the years. I'm not looking for some idea of progress or progression but rather for a sort of eclecticism or irrationality which come through in the idea of the rhizosphere.

L: Have you followed the developments of the Palace's decor?

E: Unfortunately I believe it has all been destroyed. We haven't been back because we were very attached to Fabrice Emaer.

> *L: Let's come back to the now somewhat legendary exhibition at Jansen's on Rue Royale in 1981. Even today, the* Chaise Barbare *is still sitting in the studio like a throne!*

E: After one year of 'wild' design, we drew a first collection that swept away all the cultural contribution made by the past centuries since we started back from the principles of the origin of civilizations. We've had about fifteen objects and pieces of furniture made in Italy. Then came in 1981 the exhibition at Jansen's, a magnificent traditional decoration store. Its manager, Jeanne Gambert de Loche, greeted us within the framework of the parties of the Rue Royale in the most beautiful salon. The malaise, the destabilization was immediately to be felt. The usual public was taken aback, shocked by the iron cages, the overly heavy and cumbersome *Barbare* chair, the Willendorf Venuses with their provocative buttocks. But for the press, it was so new! Our work was heralded by an outstanding reaction from the press! With even a double page in the New York Times. Hijacking? Fashion phenomenon? Everything began. Our second exhibition took place in a gallery, at Claudine Breguet's. There was no other place for us to exhibit our work. What interested us was a choice of forms and materials: two materials were used in opposition, one in the rough/untreated, the other worked on. They were very heavy, rather impractical objects which for some people seemed to evoke Zen furniture, using rocks and creating a new exoticism. We were already eliminating the theatrical aspect from our work particularly with the *Rochers* table and lamp—objects which predate by far Branzi's Domestic Animals, as Raymond Guidot has correctly pointed out. Certain design tendencies from the late seventies and early eighties, particularly in Italy, sought the rejection of heavy-industrial techniques and a new relationship to craftsmanship.

L: Could you come back to the term 'barbarian'—which is undeniably topical?

Mattia Bonetti (M): We came up with the word 'barbarian' by chance. In the first collection, there was a *Chaise Barbare* which struck the imagination of journalists. Later, we took up the title of a poem by Constantin Cavafy, 'En attendant les Barbares'. Periodically, on the inside of very sophisticated systems, there were expressions and primitive evocations. I also thought of the Arte Povera or even of Barry Flanagan's first works. Facts never crop up by chance. The apes and the monolith in the film *2001 A Space Odyssey* influenced me a lot. There is an indetermination; and I really like metaphysical questions to remain unanswered.

L: There is an intriguing detail concerning the simplicity of the materials in the barbarian collection: for the metal pieces, why did you always choose bronze-patinated iron instead of leaving the iron raw.

E: Our initial desire was really to use bronze. When that became financially possible, real bronze was cast for our objects. From then on, the iron of our creations was never patinated again: it was left as it was.

L: Was the chair redone in bronze?

E: Never, always in bronze-patinated iron.

L: In the book, 1000 Chairs *put out by Taschen, there were two of yours. Which ones were they?*

E : The *Chaise Barbare*.

L: And another one which is better enhanced by the page layout.

E: I find chairs the most difficult things to do successfully and I don't think we have ever really done a successful chair. On the other hand, there is the

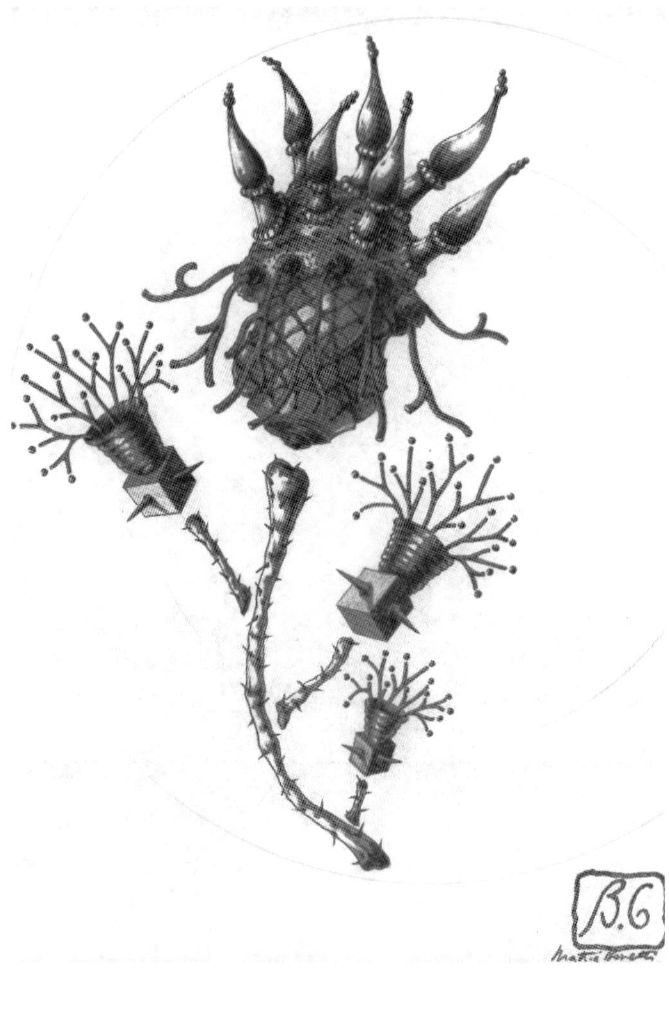

Drawing: Mattia Bonetti, 1992
pattern for a white and blue Vincennes china table set *Étranges végétations*
Ed. Objet Insolite

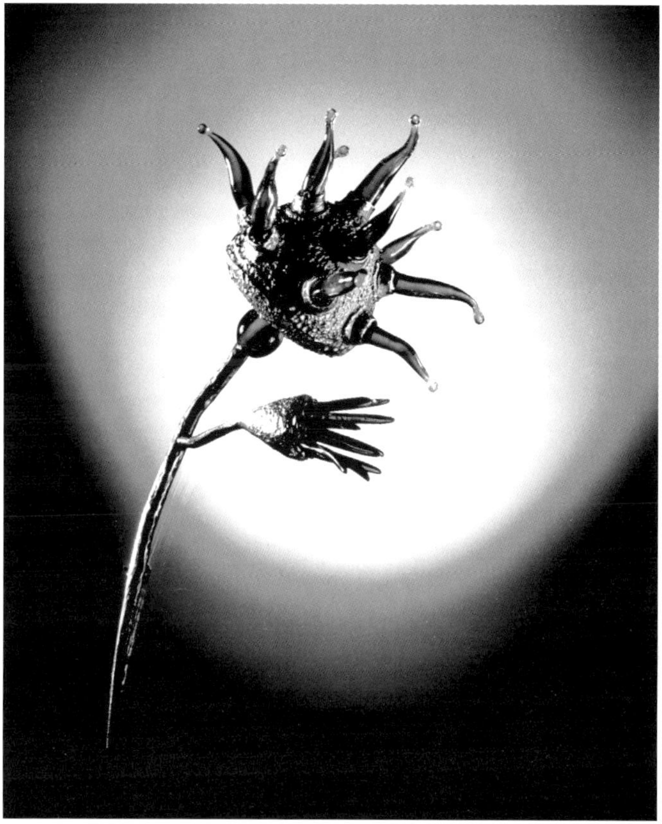

Strange Flower, brooch, 1992
blackened silver, almandin red, green turmalin, citrin, 10 cm
Ed. Best Friends.(Bad, Essen, Germany)

idea of the chair—in which case I quite like the *Prince Impérial* in painted wood and raffia.

L: That's the one that the Fiells, the authors, did actually choose.

E: Certainly not for its function. Which proves that in spite of everything a chair is linked to aesthetics. It's a chair which looks like a totem, a sculpture. Around a table, a minimum of eight light chairs are required—they have to be practical and inexpensive. In this domain, we never had the opportunities to seriously work on a seat with the industrial world. Our seats remain quite simply nice stories, like those imagined for Napoleon III's son's campaign against the Zulu: neither very practical nor very decorative.

L: Which chairs do you like best?

E: That all depends on the moment. I like some of Herbst's creations - my first design purchase at Ecart's- some of Bertoia's, some of Meda's...

L: More generally speaking, what is your relationship to contemporary art?

E: In addition to having a great personal interest, I actually live with an artist so I'm very familiar with the milieu. Gerard and I travel extensively to see exhibitions. I remember seeing great shows at the museum of decorative arts, notably on the Arte Povera. I was completely fascinated by a sack of potatoes, some of which were in bronze. Penone's and Merz's works interest me a great deal, as does 'art brut' in a different sense. At the beginning, it wasn't so easy for me to go into a gallery. The first shock came at an exhibition at Templon's, on Rue Bonaparte. He was showing half-open, rotting bananas on shelves.

L: Quite apart from living with an artist, do you collect works or reproductions of works by contemporary artists?

E: I don't buy anything that has a price or a value attached to it because I have no possessive instinct. For me, possessing is closely related to the idea of death. I like to have that distance which assures that a craving is never satisfied. That, in my opinion, is what is known as 'desire'—which differs in an important way from 'need'.

L: In the German book on your creative work, you referred to the works of those artists which highlight the furniture environment: Beuys, Braque, Matisse and so on. And you placed one of Mattia's works between Brancusi and Koons. Isn't that an allegory of your work, on a path between minimalism and kitsch?

E: Absolutely!

L: Mattia, could you tell us about your relationship to contemporary art?

M: I don't situate myself as an artist when I create furniture: I think the techniques are so entirely different. My medium of predilection used to be photography: large prints on canvas or reworked paper, that is, repainted or retouched. The subjects were invented: cities as theater sets or somewhat erotic scenes or still-lifes. One day, a journal wanted a four-handed work—already back then!—A writer and I came up with a story which could be put into images and which turned into a small exhibition. I stopped for the very simple reason that I chose the activity which worked best. For a while, I continued in both directions. I showed at Samia Saouma's gallery: there were a few sales. I kept the works in the cellar with all the original documents which had helped put these little worlds together. I go to see exhibitions, but conceptual art speaks to me less directly. As a matter of fact, I had never lived with a television image until three years ago, so I really prefer painting. I loved the Christine Borland show, there was a whole installation which played with the shadows. I had done a series of works on shadows. I have a number of Gerard Garouste's works at home;

listen to some pretty diverse music along the same lines as our creative work. I brought back music from India, Arabian music from a trip to Syria. I also have a lot of cultural activities with La Source.

L: And Mattia?

M: That's changed a lot since I have had children. I read books for my children. When I get home, I'm often tired so unfortunately I don't read much. In bed, after ten minutes, I fall asleep. I read novels or historical treatises. As for dance, I regularly go to see Forsythe. I listen to opera, sometimes obsessively for six months at a stretch; every morning, when the girls go off to school, I put on opera very loudly for twenty minutes or so. Otherwise I like the ethnic music that I buy in the most amateurish way in airports on the basis of the cover!

L: Has the fact of having children influenced your work?

E: No. I have always been very closely connected to the world of children: reliving my own mysteries and fears through my children somewhat demystified my anxieties. My sons are grown up—they are eighteen and twenty-four—and so they have a different outlook; they bring me a bit of fresh air and when they look at my work, they ask a lot of questions. At times, I find their outlook very bourgeois!

M: In my own case, I can't say that my two girls condition my way of working. I did however go and give a talk on my work at their school and it lasted three hours instead of one!

L: Haven't you ever wanted to teach?

E: It is a recurrent request to which we respond in a homeopathic way. I would really like to get into teaching through La Source. When I have a bit more time, I would like to get closer in touch with the world of children.

M: Teaching means already knowing and I feel that as someone self-taught,

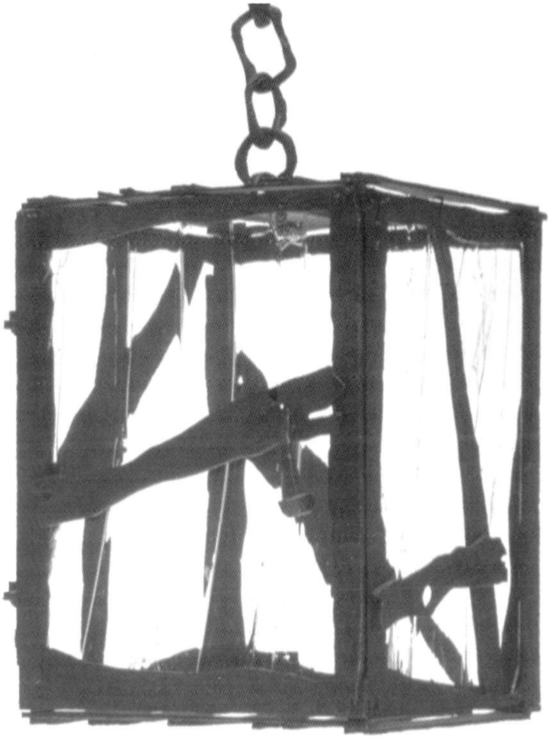

Lantern, 1996
(Hydra Collection) bronze with black patina, glass, 53x40x43 cm
Ed. David Gill Gallery (London)
Phot: Daniel Kessler

I just don't have the level. A state of mind does not suffice for teaching. Tackling problems as an amateur is impossible. If you're self-taught, you undertake things and see them through. I went through a Bauhaus-based school: the first year, the whole class spent a month drawing black strokes on a sheet; after that, it was little dots, first in pencil and then with a pen. It was really obsessional and methodical training, a long way from design. Then it was colors theory, which I think is indispensable. The only works I insist upon from my daughters are studies after nature—and I am very severe. Straightjackets are very important—even just as something to free yourself from.

L: Is your collaboration more like a duel or a duo?

E: Both; it's also a stimulation, which might from time to time be a sign of some laxness on my part; it's easy not to sign an object, because it exists in relationship to itself. It's not a performance. On the days the shows open, I always have the impression I haven't done anything, that nothing belongs to me. But at the same time there is a confrontation because you don't feel like giving up your place to the other person. It's also a game of hide-and-seek, with the double desire of wanting both to exist and to disappear.

N: Do you think being a woman has played a role in the way you work?

E: I believe that as a creative pair, our roles are rather reversed, in other words I have a more masculine role. My creative input is more along the lines of 'art brut': rougher, heavier and more provocative. The more refined side is Mattia's work.

N: Has there never been any temptation at any time to sign objects alone?

E: Sometimes... It happened. When the objects are in a gallery, people don't think about who created what. It's part of the magic of our creations.

N: What are the subjects you're most liable to argue about?

E: Sometimes there is a power relationship, but there are fundamentally no subjects on which we are completely opposed. I really think there has been a subconscious complicity right from the beginning.

N: What has your favorite commission been?

E: What I really enjoyed was the recognition after ten years of having our own style, enabling us to move on to doing industrial projects.

N: Do you have a better relationship to the customers than Mattia?

E: It's give and take, it all depends on the customers.

L: Looking over what has been published about you, I was struck by your different hairstyles over a twenty-year period. Is there any connection there with your professional life?

E: I am very flattered that you noticed any sort of evolution at all. I had straight hair and a bob since I was a little girl and I just got fed up with it! I often tried to let my hair grow, my dream being to have beautiful long curly hair, sometimes done up in a chignon like Grace Kelly. For years my attempts were fruitless, so back I went to a bob. After three years, I'd had enough of it again. I am today in a new phase with shorter and more fluffy hair. It is a personal evolution, a way of seeing life differently with fewer constraints. I go to the hairdresser in my village in Normandy. Gerard hollers sometimes when I come out but for one thing I learn all about the goings-on in the village, and for another, the hairdresser is the cousin of a critic at Art Press, so the shop is actually pretty hip.

N: You went from red to brown?

E: I experimented a fair amount with red, my hair was even carrot red.

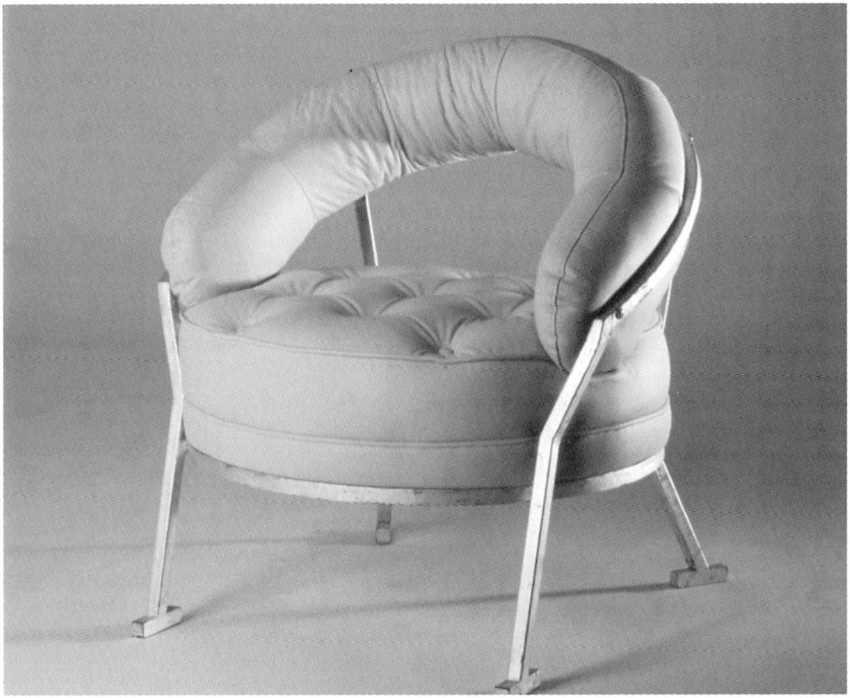

Shell, seat, 1994
gilded metal and leather, 77x73x56 cm
Ed. Neotu (Paris)
Phot: Neotu

N: Did your clothes change along with your hair?

E: I think it's all subconscious: I don't say to myself, "I'm going to do this or that". I feel a lot more relaxed.

L: You are both always very well dressed like an ideal couple, particularly in magazines. Are your clothes in phase with your creative work?

E: They are two different worlds. We did however do a chest-of-drawers in homage to Rei Kawakubo. As a piece of furniture, it has a Japanese Zen side: it's a very refined form and you can see the traces of the gold leafing on it.

L: In your work, are you the one who looks after the world of textiles?

E: I feel at ease in the world of colors: I feel more at ease there than in volumes, but Mattia is very gifted for textiles because he went to a specialized school and spent at least ten years drawing cloth. We were in Germany recently in an extraordinary, completely automated weaving factory, where they use amazing combinations of materials, and the management asked us to do a collection with hundreds of different threads.

L: When you visit a factory like that, what do you think of the relations at the heart of your trajectory between artistic techniques and industry?

E: I think the ideal is that the two coexist side by side; it's a shame that all this know-how is disappearing. I don't find plastic more beautiful than ceramic. The techniques of art could be a focal point of industrial research.

L: Recently, Gérard Garouste did stained-glass windows for a church in Burgundy. It has always been the Ministry of Arts's wish to get artists into collaboration with the world of artisans and craftspeople in order to create a dialectic between the two so they might mutually enrich one another. Do you have the same feeling between yourselves and the world of artisans?

E: I often wonder about this question: should this sort of manual know-how be continued today? Is it the last burst of an era fated to disappear because the work is unique, specific and contrary to industry? But I think that in working at the same time with craftspeople and industry, we raise the problematic. Once again, there is no single, cut-and-dried path, there is only the essential: the questioning process.

L: Have you worked for the Ministry of Arts?

M: Under Jack Lang, we did the lights and the entry console at the ministry. We brought along our own artisans. At the time, we were just starting out. Thanks to the public commissions policy of the delegation for plastic arts, we were then able to do a beautiful and poetic footbridge in Quimper in homage to Max Jacob. We also recently worked for Mobilier National. They didn't know what the final destination of our work was going to be, so they talked about a waiting room for an institutional site. For everything artisanal, they are just excellent. We were really impressed. There is this extraordinary worker who runs the metal shop.

E: There is an anecdote about this waiting room. The requirement was: "whatever you do, don't use silk because people get so scared while they're waiting that they sweat enormously, and they leave marks on the couches!" Of course we used silk!

M: There is a couch, two armchairs, a coffee table, a rug and a beautiful console. We were tested on the basis of a first series. I guess the results must have seemed fairly good as we went along because they proceeded to order

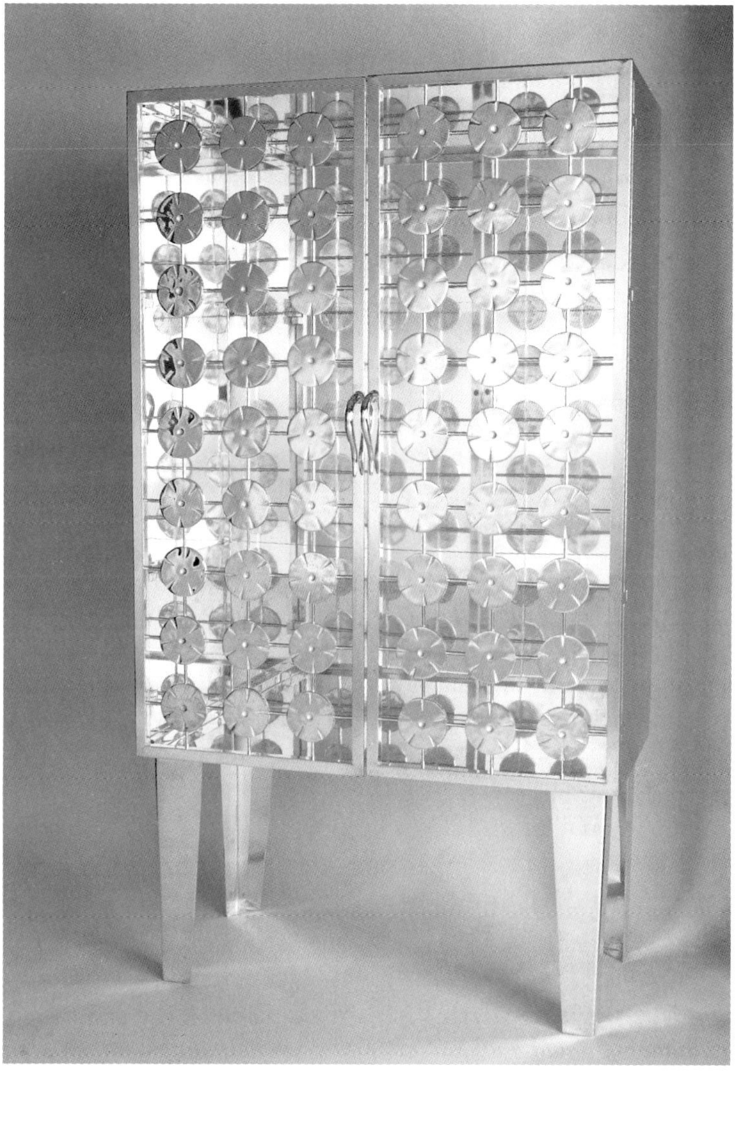

Flowers in the air, cabinet, 1994
silver plated metal and bronze, 82x150x40 cm
Ed. David Gill Gallery (London)

a desk and a lamp. There is a unity between the using of an ebony veneer, cast aluminum and nickel-plated metal gilded in gold leaf. Amongst the colors, there are browns almost as black as the ebony; the velvet of the silk is very black and the white and gold metals have been worked almost like the body of a car: it doesn't have an artisanal look; it is very refined and exacting. The forms of the whole are very geometrical. We were very involved in the studios. They called us for the slightest detail and the slightest decision they had to make. There was a veritable exchange and they are very well equipped!

L: Had you already worked with the Manufacture de Sèvres?

M: A long time ago, we had a grant to work with Sèvres. Instead of producing a traditional dinner service, we imagined a contemporary Marie-Antoinette who would have wished to integrate porcelains into a piece of furniture. We had thus made an orange and blue cabinet: eight copies of the *Cabinet de Sèvres* were produced, and were all sold. The collaboration was a catastrophe: we had to keep plying the caster with bottles of wine just to get him to work. They are a year late on the commissions; in studios where they should have had forty, they only had four. The work is in every way sumptuous. Especially a top on the upper part which is a genuine technical achievement. They had to make objects especially just so it could withstand a number of firings. Since the first cabinet we did for Jansen, we have always continued to use terracotta, working with a full range of more or less natural colors. Our last collection at Neotu's includes terracotta objects. All told, that makes dozens of objects.

E: I think we are the most prolific designers around with an incalculable number of pieces of furniture and objects! We do an enormous number of private jobs that people never see and each time we create original pieces, sometimes by the hundreds. We're working on an exhaustive catalogue of our work. It has become indispensable to see more clearly. We have kept our most important drawings, but unfortunately almost no photographs

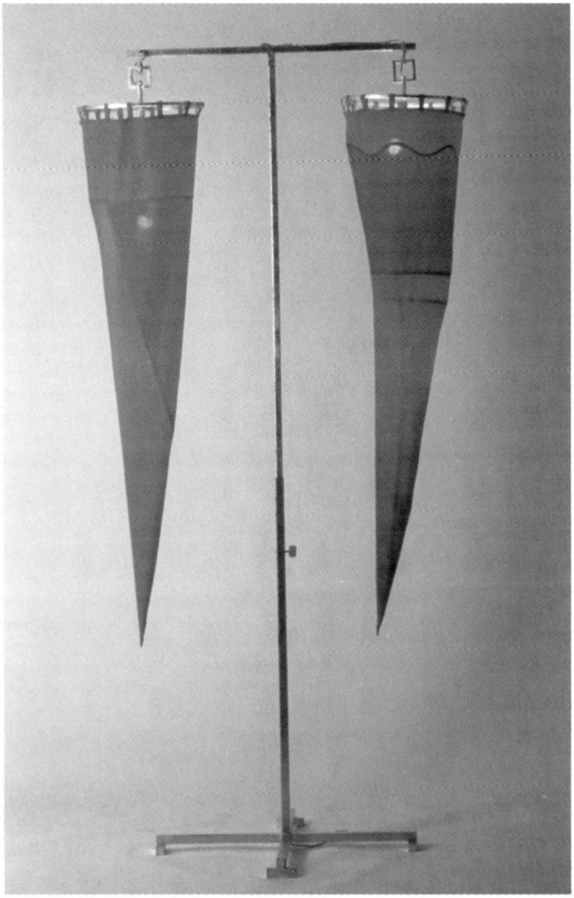

Oriflamme, standard lamp, 1994
metal, gilded with a white gold leaf, silk, 220x110x75 cm
Ed. Neotu (Paris)
Phot: Neotu

because the pieces of furniture go from one artisan to the next without passing through our studio, and then straight to the customer. We have a lot of jobs abroad to which we do not travel. We had a complete apartment delivered to Hong Kong for one of the children of our customer. We saw the finished objects but not the installation. That doesn't bother me: "where there's no bother, there's no pleasure." The most beautiful and certainly the most exciting moment is that of conception. The most boring part is when you are actually building something because you have to look after so many details. When you invent, you dream. During the realization phase, we are sometimes agreeably surprised and sometimes a little disappointed. Time, today, just doesn't permit you, economically, to go everywhere and supervise everything. In a contract, a return trip for verification is not included: imagine we went to Orleans to the cabinet-maker's with whom we work; today, we see two pieces of furniture. But for the same client, we are actually imagining fifty-odd pieces: we'd virtually have to go see him fifty times; same thing for the glass-maker, and so on. It's just not feasible. On the other hand, we have an enormous phone and fax budget.

N: Could you describe your adventures with 'Mr. Tiger'?

M: He's Japanese, one of the biggest collectors of tigers in the world. He lives surrounded by more than two-thousand objects representing tigers of all sizes. One day he went to Hermès. He absolutely wanted to have a full set of luggage with a tiger design: they refused. He is a very original character, always dressed in tiger clothes; he's fifty-some years old. Thanks to a mutual friend, we created about twenty objects for his new apartment. He had just come into an inheritance. Those are the kinds of commissions we just cherish, with magnificent material that costs 1400 dollars a yard. We didn't know what to do at the end because we had to put tiger everywhere—hand-stitched, in gilded and black patinated bronze, in rock crystal. He wanted a chaise longue with a rising stool so you could tan the sole of your feet! Everything was done in France and then exported. It takes about a year to produce objects of that level of sophistication. We show the drawings and then the technical study: if the customer is in agreement, we can quickly do an exact estimate and set to work.

N: There was also the English woman you had as a customer?

M: She slaps her chest with both hands and proudly proclaims, "I am working class!" She's about fifty and met a more elderly Greek who had made a fortune in oil and who had a great collection of art from the time of his first marriage. A great love was born and she gave him something very important: the son he never had. They sold the collection of impressionists at the height of the market and bought some more recent art instead. She very intelligently acquired some late-period Picassos on the wise advice of Alexandre Iolas. The woman and her husband decided to create a foundation in Greece on Hydra, inaugurated by an exhibition of our work: she entirely produced the collection. Her decorator was Jacques Grange. She wanted to have more strictly contemporary surroundings, so she called on us to work first in London and then in Athens. She has reliable taste, which is not always the case for that sort of clientele. She is fairly assertive and sometimes when we would show her drawings, she would scarcely look at them—that's what's so funny! There are no lack of people with money. But you could count on your fingers the ones with her profile; they all know one another. In London, she has an apartment and in Athens a small, late-neoclassical mansion. We had to work in conjunction for the hanging of the works. The scale was smaller in Athens: she wanted a Greco-Turkish style. It's a pleasure to work with people like her.

For the London part, Jacques Grange had already thought of the material and the colors, so we stuck to that same vein. We furnished a lot with extraordinary creations such as four different entry consoles, and the furnishings in her bedroom. There is a series of fur-fringed rugs for her hallway and we said to ourselves that she was liable to trip over them; but as it turns out, it works very well. She insisted on having a throne! At the same time, we are not 'objectists'. For example, in Hong Kong, we conceived everything. In our trade, it is very easy to lose your sense of things and go right off the rails. Which is why I find it fairly good now and again to give oneself a mental structure. It is important in off-balance situations to maintain notions of balance. We cannot always be in disorder and permanent desire. In our creative work, there is the idea of a family and the development of a structure: it's indispensable.

L: Are the lamps all part of a family?

M: The *Lune* lamp is probably the object which best symbolizes us along with the *Chaise Barbare*. It is a small bronze lamp somewhere between Brancusi and Africa. The disk might make you think of the comic book 'Tintin et le Temple du soleil'. There is no particular technicity about it. It continues to sell: it has become a classic. The *Émail* lamp was a commission from the Limoges enamel biennial where we first worked by doing two small tables; the lamp is made entirely out of enameled metal. It's a satellite, something like a lunar module. It has no motif. The enamel covers it completely like a casserole—in the most noble sense, because it was very precious enamel! The *Oriflamme* standard lamp is a large, vertical and fairly sober object, minimalist and fairly big with two large cones of patched cloth, like an air handle which ends in a sewn-up tip that hangs down. It has to do with the rapport between a fluid thing—the rather light and very brightly colored silks—and a very stable object. The *Fake Pair* lamp stems from our love for the idea of resembling each other without being exactly the same, being fraternal twins. You're a brunette, I'm blond, you've got two boys, I've got two girls. To come back to the *Oriflamme*, as soon as we tackle forms of a certain size in three dimensions, we easily fall back into a relatively sculptural universe, somewhat beyond design strictly speaking. For instance, the *Atoll* cupboard is part of a more modernist collection with more refined forms—like peanuts, Viallat-style, like fried eggs, painters' palettes of spermatozoa.

L: Speaking of spermatozoa, could you describe your experience in the field of cigars?

M: We drafted the inside of a cigar shop in Beverly Hills on Rodeo Drive. It's not a chain yet, but the headquarters. The owner is French; he has been living in the States for twenty years and has made it producing small gold jewelry. He wanted to diversify his activities. So he launched a new line of cigars, called *Aristoff*. The decor we did is the consequence!

L: Along the same lines, I very much like the Fastabend piece which reminds me of the world of curiosity cabinets.

E: It is, above all, a super piece of furniture for putting things away. It's a dream to have a single piece and to be able to put everything in it: every component was thoroughly studied right down to the most minute details. It's expensive because there is an insane amount of work, but it's very well finished on the inside. We got the job from a German manufacturer working on a program of luxury walk-in closets: the commission was for the creation of a normalized and modulable system. If you have a room set aside for the purpose, they come and do the shelving to measure. For the commission, we used Buren-style stripes. When I worked for Tilbury, I had asked Mattia to get involved in some of the creations, and he used black and white stripes. The *Bobine* cupboard also has stripes. We think there is a lot of humor and derision in our creations. Which is not to say that we actually laugh a lot during the manufacturing process. But we like our objects to be vested with a smile. It does happen that we just explode with laughter in front of a piece of furniture. Design is sometimes boring. But the *Prince Impérial* chair is pure humor: the imaginary furnishings of Napoléon III's son at war with the Zulu. The *Barbare* chair is typically of the same register. The house in Hong Kong is a wink of the eye at the idea of reinterpreted chinoiserie: humor again. It is difficult to imagine a Chinese living in a decor of revisited chinoiseries—but he has a sense of humor! You need a triple dose to do a job of that kind. The *Cabinet de Sèvres* cupboard is pure derision held at a distance. We really went for it. We're not ethnologists. Sometimes the whole thing falls on its face: we just about got to do a large decor job for Cartier at the Cannes festival last year for instance, but there is heavy moral pressure these days. It was for a gala dinner, the steps were like false diamonds! The *Dreaming Room* we did for Philips is also based on humor. It is part of a project which was launched during the Berlin international fair to create a space on a gigantic stand: for us, it was obviously the bedroom! We had created a very lunar atmosphere and the only technological device was a television positioned like a meteorite.

L: Could you tell us about the Pastor apartment, one of your most recent creations?

E: It was thanks to the Neotu Gallery that we met this collector of contemporary art. We started working on a relatively big apartment near the Eiffel Tower, used mostly by his two daughters, both students. We did a room for one of the girls—using a daisy motif—part of the furnishing in the living room and a few pieces of furniture in the dining room, library and the smaller, more intimate sitting room. In that particular case, we went to visit the site, discussed their taste and often instead of doing a single project, we would propose two. With the Pastors, we decided to go with a heady decor because they have classical furniture of extremely high quality. The refurbishment was overseen by the antique-dealer Gismondi. Next to them, our creations have to stand up—otherwise the whole thing is for naught.

L: And the house in Hong Kong?

M: It was one of our biggest jobs. We had carte blanche and total budgetary freedom. At the beginning, it was like standing at the edge of a precipice. We had already worked for them; we did their private mansion in London. Then there was a commission for offices and their boat. The rapport with the local architects was very important because we had to work in an

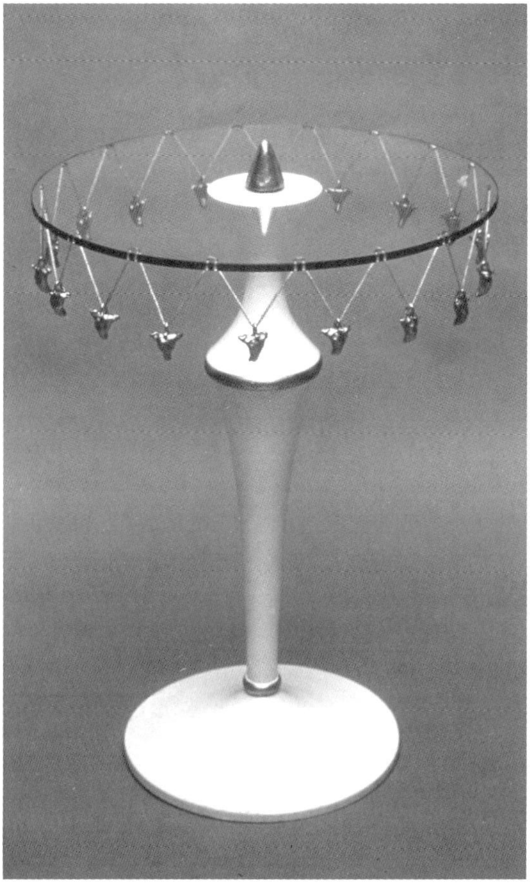

India, pedestal table, 1986
lacquered wood, gild, gilded bronze and glass, 84x60 cm
Ed. Neotu (Paris)
Phot: Karin Knoblich

already existent house. There were a lot of architects, but they were quite ineffectual. We had redone the interior painting four times over and they hadn't even finished the exterior. The entrance gate had identical floral motifs on all the balconies. The house is on the peak, and so is on a split-level: you are forever going up and down. We used a special marble, certain types of wood that recur in all our work and some metal parts. They live in a family so the children's apartments are in the same house on the lower floors, a little more 'prêt-à-porter' style. All the rooms are unique. The painters who came from Paris stayed five months on the site. The furniture was sent out from France. The motorboat was built in Italy, the first of a series of one-hundred-twenty-foot yachts. Our decoration was very sober. We took the opposite tack from the usual sort of marine decoration, which usually involves a surfeit of bad taste and luxurious details. We made reference to the boats of the American films of the 1950s with simplicity and glamour. The job brought good luck because the boat stayed several months at the shipyard. And when some English clients visited the shipyard where they were having their own boat constructed, they wanted the same decoration. Unfortunately, it didn't stay moored there long enough for us to get a third contract!

L: Did you install a chimney like on Starck's pinnace?

M: No!

L: What did you get out of the experience of the garden furniture you made with the help of the Limousin regional council?

M: A regional company specializing in chestnut headed up the operation. We worked together with a barrel-maker, a glass-maker and an artisan who did the metal and log work. The manufactured objects remained at the prototype stage because there was no commercial distribution. However, once again V.I.A. got involved and normally should have played an interface role with the industry. The people who had commissioned the work must have simply said to themselves that it was some sort of publicity operation for the region. As a matter of fact, we don't even know what has become of our furniture. In the same region, we had already worked in Aubusson with two manufacturers. For the recycled-glass container, on the other hand, things were very clear: they told us it was only a project on paper to kick-start a campaign around large urban garbage containers. Our project was the most serious of all for once. As we often do, we proposed two fairly different tracks, one fairly strict—a gray parallelepiped, like a rock crystal— and the other distinctly more glamorous, a big pink mushroom with motifs in black wrought iron and flower-form mouths.

N: Conversely, is the Montpellier tramway for you a leap into industrial realization?

E: After the dossier was picked, we had three weeks to do the tramway. We had made three propositions for the outside and a single inside. They didn't choose the most audacious but the most anecdotal with the motif of a swallow. They were afraid of public reaction. But sticking swallows onto public transport is already a sort of provocation. Moreover, the world of design was rather surprised! I've got no worries, as soon as the tramway runs, people will like it. The interior, on the other hand, generates general enthusiasm. It is fairly difficult to really do something because changing even the smallest element is a heavy process, especially in light of security constraints; but we have managed to change the seats and hand rail, to create molds for certain pieces. Most of the time, we went for the most simple. We opted for a fairly particular coloration and fairly soft forms while in the initial project everything was very square. The inside is perhaps a bit feminine. We wanted it to be user-friendly, almost sensual. We had really wanted a vaulted, sky-like ceiling. Unfortunately it was made out of flat-folded sheet metal. We also wanted to put in fairly intimate lighting. It wasn't possible. But we did get what was essential. In that sort of market, there are proposals with which one has to me prepared to be flexible and others on which one has to be intransigent. We worked directly with Alsthom. I figure they were delighted to get out of the study bureau they had been associated with for a number of years. They were at loggerheads and unable to work together; but in fact, thanks to our experience, they are going to be able to enable cities constructing tramways to personalize their mode of transport. In these types of enterprises, everything is clean while at your wall-paperers, it's ten times dirtier. Its high-quality make-shift on a giant scale. We're Alice in Wonderland. I think this order is going to lead to the same sort of kick-off as with Nina Ricci. We provide a freshness that people don't allow themselves. I think they are going to say, "hey, why don't we add a little touch of freedom?" That's what's interesting; we're little troublemakers.

L: Was your experience with Nina Ricci a total success?

E and M: The decision to pick us was made by Mr. Fuchs, former president of the company and a collector of contemporary art. But he didn't approach us as such but rather as a business man. We knew from the outset that he had a level of understanding which is uncommon in his milieu, in France at any event, because in Italy and Germany, many business leaders are involved in creation. In my opinion, it is a very French deficiency. The experiment lasted about five years. They started out with nothing in terms of beauty and make-up products; they had perfumes like *L'Air du temps* but no line of care and cosmetic products; so it was very important for them because, economically, that represents an enormous production and communication investment. Ricci's image was a bit out of date: it too was a story to be created. The idea of calling upon people like us who were neophytes in the domain enabled them to come up with a much broader vision, simply because we did not fall into any pre-established system. We began with the *Teint Ricci*, the name of an entire product range. There was to no longer be any gap for the woman using it between caring for her skin and applying her make-up—it was to be one seamless gesture: the other brands created a discontinuity between the two. There were no rigid guidelines or specifications. We didn't have the feeling that any very sophisticated market survey had been carried out. Just a woman with a head on her shoulders; not a fashion victim, but someone truly free and independent. She comes from the feminist revolution. Quite sweet actually, which is why we chose pastels right off the bat. They provided the product quantities and types; for lipstick, for instance, there are six presentation systems. Sensuality and ergonomics were at the very heart of our reflections. The basic idea is rooted in nature. The little twists are to some extent our signature. They conjure up the feet of the 'Boulle' chest-of-drawers or a ziggurat. We have always worked with clay: its suppleness and form corresponds to a hand gesture, the primal gesture: after all, the kneading and twisting of clay are very primitive gestures. It has to be said that they weren't asking us for an anonymous product; they didn't want to eliminate the designers' style—which is rare in this line of work. On the contrary, they pushed us right to the forefront; the big cosmetics houses usually have their own integrated services or else they contract out to big structures. For communications purposes, the company still mentions Garouste and Bonetti, and some of their objects are signed. In the perfume field, we did have a small project which backfired on us: the first juice for Lacroix for whom we drafted the haute couture salons. We were the object of a decision beyond our control. We didn't feel responsible for the failure in any way. When they produced the juice, they didn't even consult Lacroix! For Ricci, the juice was developed in parallel; we used three colors in keeping with the perfume's strength: eau de toilette, parfum de toilette and perfume. Then there were the derived bathroom products, featuring excrescences corresponding to surface bumps making them easier to hold on to. The golden flame-shaped bottles call to mind the world of elves. We wanted to communicate this marvelousness to the consumer. We really tried to work the materials; instead of using glass or some noble materials for cosmetic products, we chose plastics to recreate the luminosity, flash and transparency. They needed to extend their range so we created variants on one continuous theme—as we often do in our work. Then they wanted

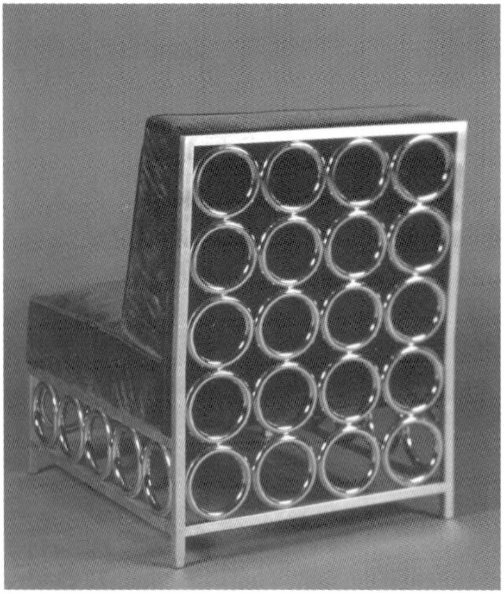

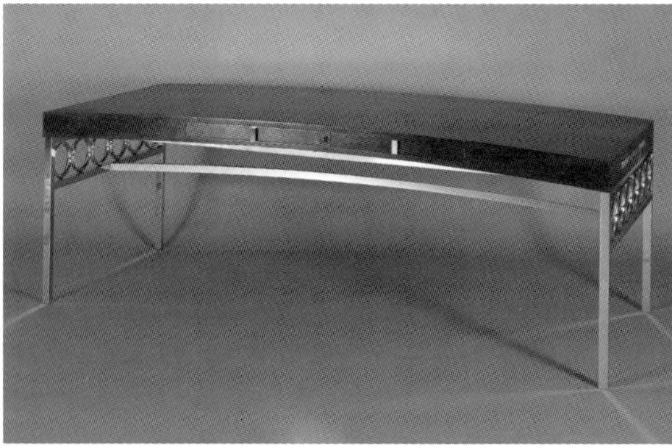

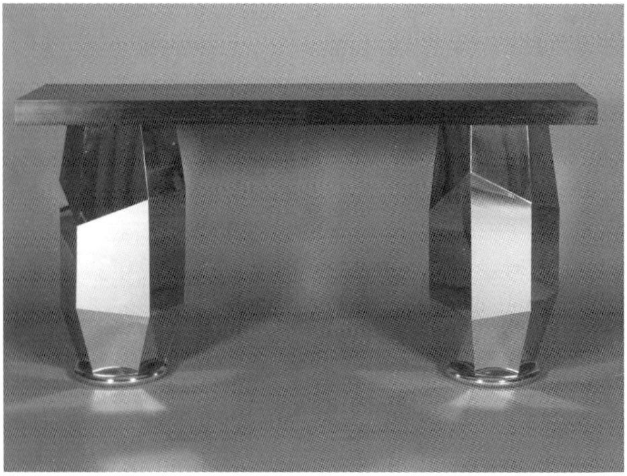

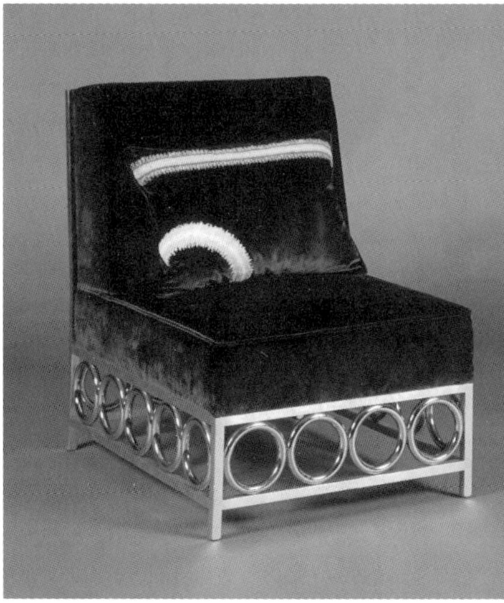

Creations for the Mobilier National, 1997
- low armless chair (back and front) : gilded and chromium-plated metal, embroided silk velvet, 68x90x88 cm
- console table, 175x100x50 cm; desk, 220x75x98 cm : gilded and chromium-plated metal, Macassar ebony veneer top

Prototypes from the research and creation studio, Mobilier National collections.
Pictures from the Mobilier National
Phot : I. Bideau

to make a perfume for adolescents; so we started out in a different direction. The bottle alludes to Alice's cat, to twirling dervishes and so on. It makes up a whole which is a sort of cultural game. The *Belles de Ricci* cork is a flower—one of the principal ingredients of perfumes; over all, we wanted to bring out the idea of luxury, but without the luxury; it's a way of de-dramatizing luxury, taking away its pompous side and its immediately recognizable look. For us, and for them, the operation was a success. The spirit in which the lines were done was even copied in malls by other brands!

L: What do you make of your recent experience with Les Trois Suisses?

E and M: It fits into the continuum of the adventure the company has been involved in over the past several years with fashion setters as well as designers. They bring out two catalogues a year and they wanted us to come up with a line of household objects, taking account of the fact that it was for a mail-order catalogue. The objects have to be easy to take apart; everything has to be able to go into packing cases. The clientele is middle class, so costs have to be kept down. We had total freedom. The end product was a sort of nomadic collection: furniture which can be built, folded, unfolded, and which is targeted at a young consumer group. It is unfortunate because the consumers, who need a while to figure out the nature of a project, are unable to find the products from one season to the next. They paid for the prototypes but not for the research work. Les Trois Suisse's material of predilection is textile. Which, in terms of objects, leads to a tent—twenty years after the sails in the Palace. It is something out of Medieval illuminations showing people going off to war. Like the flags of the time, the tent is done with bright colors. It obviously makes a person think of the orient. It is designed to recreate an atmosphere which can be put up and taken down quickly. It is a way of secluding oneself without being completely isolated. Beyond that, of course, there were some necessary and indispensable features: we based our work on certain items in their catalogue such as this fold-away bed to which we added cushions, a quilted spread and our little varnished and lathe-turned wooden feet resembling those on Madame Récamier's bed. A person can have guests without having the impression of having someone in their room. One of the most important objects is a small portable lamp whose inspiration comes from work-site lamps; its little hooks allow it to be attached anywhere. They also help hold the tent up. We chose orange and black in reference to Greece. For Les Trois Suisses, the two pages featuring the work of creators is more of an advertising venture than a commercial reality: we were instrumentalized and we accept that.

L: What do you think about the world of design publishing and distribution in France.

M: After twenty years in the trade, I have the feeling there are two realities which don't communicate: industry and galleries. Sometimes industry comes to take a look at the world of galleries as if it were a window onto the exclusive. It is through the gallery world that we came to be recognized. It is impossible to interest a gallery in creating a molded-plastic chair. On the other hand, if we want to build a piece of furniture out of elaborate clays, we can go through a gallery. In industry, the artisanal dimension only exists in the case of a prototype. The gallery curtails our creations in a somewhat formal fashion and prevents us from using certain materials. But there is an enormous advantage in that too: the gallery fosters the imagination. It brings in an elite clientele because the products are rather expensive. We have three principal galleries, Neotu and En attendant les barbares in Paris and David Gill in England. A couple of foreign galleries sort of gravitate around them, limiting themselves to reselling the work. With the first three, we do an exhibition of new pieces every two years and they fast-track us on to new jobs. There are no contracts or anything, it's based on friendship. In any case, there are far too few galleries in France which meet the financial responsibility of their choices. And even when they do, they always maintain the option of replacing one creator with another, while we of course have no such equivalent possibility. On top of which, the gallery system often imposes an opaqueness—particularly financial—which does not always foster full confidence.

L: What is your relationship to nature?

E: It's sort of a leitmotif of our creative work. Nature is very present; I have a country house with a garden full of flowers and a vegetable patch. I really like the Citroën, Giverny, Albert Kahn and Bagatelle gardens as well as the Irish countryside; in Japan, nature is a bit too domesticated which makes me a bit afraid. Unfortunately we've never been offered landscaping work. It's too bad because we would have been happy to collaborate with a landscaper. We created a artificial garden for an exhibition at the Cartier Foundation with architectural works and sculpted hedges; it was a pastiche of the classic French garden like a film set, the structure itself was visible.

M: There is a symbolic dimension to our relation to nature. We wanted to get back to another principle, as is often the case in our work, this time something to do with blue and white plates, the taste for which came from China and was taken up again by Delft. We wanted to create flowers but in a very precise fashion on the graphic level, like a cross-section. We wound up with *Étranges végétations*. Just imagine: you take the flower in your hands and get pricked everywhere. It was so strange that people didn't want to eat from it.

L: What is your favorite dish Elizabeth?

E: Tomato salad.

M: My favorite is pasta. Our project for Panzani never came to fruition. There was one type of pasta that brought sports to mind, another travel. We also worked for Lenôtre. We drew a charm for their Twelfth Night cakes. We worked for a chocolate company and freeze-dried products too.

L: Seeing as the noodle remained virtual, did the turtle become a conceptual object?

E: It certainly did in the sense of Jeff Koons and the curiosity cabinets. We were the ones who thought up the Louvre spoon in the shape of a woman, the Roman oil lamp and Cellini. The turtle was a commissioned piece for a Swedish multinational. Nine international designers were asked to make ashtrays for a traveling exhibition in order to get around the problems associated with advertising tobacco. We chose the turtle: an object to look at, easily identifiable, a pretext. The two live turtles in the garden of our studio arrived much later! Another influence was an object by Giulio Romano and certain plinths for monuments. The hollow of the turtle shell became the ashtray—then we decided to give it a human shape: a hybrid being with the arms of a sphinx, a type of female jogger in shorts and bandanna, something between the vegetal and the human. The same mold was used for a version in bronze and another in multicolored ceramic—like a Meissen object. Our object is to provoke people, to get them to think about taste. One of the social roles of the designer is to lead people to ask themselves questions about the form and the price of the object. It should raise questions and not necessarily be an easy thing to buy.

M: The Ricard ashtray is also one of our most playful objects: it was an advertising design so it's less provocative than the turtle. The ashtray is round, unbreakable and sufficiently deep; it's shaped like a top and returns to its initial position when tipped over. Plus it can be stacked up and costs very little because it was put out in hundreds of thousands of copies. The pitcher is very successful with already 800,000 copies made. The number of copies stolen is a sign of its success, we've even found it at antique fairs. The carafe had very precise specifications with great attention paid to the logo. We had to gentrify the brand name while maintaining the object's spirit of warm conviviality. First came the idea of a gourd—ample and round in molded glass, extra transparent—then we added on two suns. Many tests were made, one of which was for stability on a tray. Thus, the carafe was ballasted. It was designed not to drip and the water's flow rate had to be continuous. It was our first experience with computer-generated images—a fictional film ad. And this was the first time Ricard had worked with well-known designers. There is a new state of mind in French design, many advertising campaigns use design objects: Tefal, for instance, used our furniture for a frying pan ad.

L: Do the museums have this same state of mind?

E: Design is a difficult subject for the museums. Sometimes the exhibitions—like the one held recently at Beaubourg—are a bit disappointing. In fact, that mini-retrospective was put together with pieces from the collections of other museums. It didn't give a sufficiently complete idea of our work. The presentation at the Monnaie de Paris was far more elaborate. The Meymac show was also more interesting.

L: How does it feel to see the Chaise Barbare *on a plinth?*

E: It's very curious, there is a certain amount of pretension. The sale to a public collection has an ambiguous feel to it. It's flattering, that's true. But more generally, I find the purchasing policy of the museums is often too hasty—for fear of 'missing out' on the artist of the century, which occasions a certain indecisiveness, even a 'floating'.

N: While we're on the topic of floating, Mattia, do you still swim as often as before?

M: I really like the water. It really makes you feel good. I'm sorry I can't do it anymore because it helps develop concentration. I need domestic order, I don't need order at other people's. That's all tied up with anxiety and neurosis. We work face to face. We have a system for keeping things in order but we don't have mountains of material. I draw quite quickly but they take a long time to do because you have to show detailed propositions to the clients. I used to make watercolor drawings but now I don't have the time. I use Caran d'Ache pencils on standard letter-size paper which allows me to group together the major pieces of furniture in a room on the same piece of paper. There's an atmosphere. We've never sold drawings on their own but we're often asked to. I refuse because I want to keep them. They serve as our archives because we don't have any photographs. Eventually I'll give them to the state. In Germany, they printed three lithographs from the drawings. I'd like to make a selection of the drawings because it's the step I prefer. When I do the drawing for private jobs, I think a lot about the final scene and the people who are going to live there; I see it as a movie set or a publicity photo. There are no figures in the drawings because what interests me is the absence and emptiness. I think that our furniture tells a story. In the end, what is functional is often surpassed by the imagination. Our objects don't reveal their function immediately and they bring others to mind. Sometimes there are objects or parts of furniture that turn up on the drawing but don't correspond to what was commissioned. I give very little freedom to the commissioning party. I try to figure them out and prevent them from using objects I wouldn't like to see appear in their 'story'. The drawing is completed when the piece of paper is filled up. We like doing a rough psychoanalysis of our clients. We please ourselves and we please others. Our suppleness is great but without concessions. We have very few taboo subjects; I mean we could decorate the Charles de Gaulle aircraft carrier if we were asked to: military stuff is often very beautiful. Our creations are not as 'politically correct' as some: that can sometimes spoil our sleep. We're not looking to provoke any thrills the way the masters provoke pleasure, especially by drawing upon the Ancien Régime. But we have grasped the eighteenth-century spirit of privileges. However, we also work for the nouveaux riches who do buy contemporary pleasures, something the old aristocracy no longer does. We're not looking to create, through our creations, a new moralizing theoretical system.

L: What dialectic is there between the subconscious, its cultural references and your creations?

E: I believe that the subconscious is always present in everyone. I would say that there are some points that keep coming up. We are aware of creating some pretty sexual forms with less and less modesty. We reuse forms just for pleasure. In terms of structure, there is exactly the same in the *Atoll* cupboard as in the *Paradise cabinet*, in an unconscious manner. The role of the subconscious is obvious in our work but that of the structure much less so. There are fairly 'ornamented' primary forms. We get away to some extent from the straitjacket of form with the smallest objects as well as with spectacular projects like our virtual kitchen for an exhibition at the Guggenheim Museum in New York. Our objects are not especially oneiric. There is a great deal of restraint.

L: What is your analysis of the present situation of design?

M: There is an intellectual elite that is able to see, understand and promote it which is quite rare. There's another elite, the moneyed elite. Design changes according to prices. We could make one-hundred-fifty dollar objects look like 1500 dollar objects. It's a question of the outside envelope. No one gives you power, you have to take it, that's the strength of Bill Gates versus the Sultan of Brunei. In Italy, movie stars are called *divi*, in English they are stars, there is a cosmic relationship. With the death of Lady Diana comes the mourning of a type of elite. I was really touched by the image of a dump-truck full of flowers. As for prizes, we are very close to the Italian publishers who work on order without any stock, and sometimes with a nine-month wait for Le Corbusier's furniture from Cassina's. Our private clientele keeps us going, especially the liberal professionals. Just recently we created some shelving for a young doctor, an act of pure whim on his part. Our mythical clientele came after the Christian Lacroix showrooms - Princess Thurn and Taxis, for instance, who called us directly. She holds court from eight in the morning with her chamberlain. There's a demand from the international clientele for a personalized eccentricism. There's plenty of work for other creators. Why don't they do it? Perhaps they are obsessed with industry. Many major

Italian groups came to see us and then never showed any signs of life again. Some aspect of our work must have scared them off. I would have loved working in plastics with Kartell. Our career has surfed over the crisis, but we've maintained a consistency in our relationships with the artisans: we have had the same metal-worker since the beginning. We were anxious to reintroduce all different materials in order to touch the senses. We are not at war against any aesthetic movement. We act for ourselves without any will to prophesize. Our hope is to give people the feeling of freedom in the choice of forms. Good taste really bothers us a lot. What we care about is implanting doubt. We don't have any rules. Between the furniture of Gehry and Eames on the one hand and the Bauhaus experiment with plywood and folded tube on the other hand, there isn't that much revolution. What interests us is a personal and artisanal putting together of things. It's more the derivative products that call out to the designers than the furniture industry itself. Wanting to show chrome tubing is not necessarily very modern. It's more simple to sell the old ideas than the new. We're not very comfortable in Le Corbusier's couches and armchairs. You're pushed toward the back, you slide toward the front, the height of the backrest is not off. Where do you put a Le Corbusier couch in a low-cost housing project apartment? What would be interesting is to be the director of a collection at Conforama even though people are often very happy with the current production. When we won the creator's award for 1991, we were able to determine that design was just a tiny part of contemporary furniture: it's a picture of reality but not very economical. There are no more than three-hundred of us. We are a laboratory like Haute Couture. It would be especially interesting to study the work Philippe Starck did while he was at Thomson.

L: It has been suggested that your relationship to the people who commission your work is tainted with a certain amount of cynicism. What do you think about that?

M: I think it's pretty much justified. We are both very detached and acutely aware of what we are doing. But there is also another way of looking at our work: as being far more immediate, physical, almost carnal and spontaneous. If there is a cynicism, there is also a tenderness. And there is above all a lot of irony involved in being able to create. Our objects vehicle at once irony and seriousness. The ornament hides and reveals meaning: it is a part of figuration and has become structural in our work. The minimalism in Jean Nouvel's work is a sort of mask disguising technique. Bob Wilson is baroque and minimal. Beneath a rigid veneer, Rei Kawakubo is outrageous. Today what matters is a natural make-up with three tons of product. It's hypocritical.

N: What is luxury for you?

E: Luxury is the consumer's buying power. There are people who have an innate taste for luxury and who can, with very few means, make something very luxurious, or at least give that impression. Time is a real luxury.

M: I am aware of a certain bulimia in our work. I only feel good when I'm in the doing mode. We grew up in the religion of work and production. It would be sublime if a customer offered us time. To return to luxury, when we did the Haute Couture salons for Christian Lacroix, it was essentially a luxury place, projecting an image and an appearance of luxury, but with materials which were not luxurious at all, like cut branches and that sort of thing. I'm thinking of a woman who would come out of the water naked, like Ursula Andress in 'James Bond', only instead of a bathing suit, she would be covered in seaweed and pearls from the sea and corals on her head: that would be true luxury. For the Montpellier tramway, we tried to raise the image of the passenger. The idea of a square tramway always scares me a little insofar as it immediately makes me think of stereotyped working-class images. I appreciate the saying 'less is more' but it is definitely not a good line of conduct or a religion to which I adhere completely because 'less can be a bore'. It is often an excuse not to try and go the extra mile, a form of intellectual stinginess.

E: We have two profoundly different ways of operating. In our work, we really run the risk of getting snubbed, as in "they only work for the rich, and it's crass, it's ugly, it's gaudy". That's better than tirelessly repeating your whole career long, "rectangle, triangle and circle". I rally completely to the idea of multiplicity and difference like Philippe Decouflé who, in an interview, recently said: "I am in favor of a choreography using small people, fat people and big people; above all I don't have a vision of the uniform body."

M: I really like the contrasts created between a fairly ornate piece of furniture and, for instance, an immense painting by Pollock hanging behind it; on the other hand, I find it a little too obvious to put a Jasper Morrison desk in front of a painting by Ryman. It's a rather pompous attitude. I can't stand the idea of balance. It's the academicism of today. I don't think people are sufficiently aware of that. I'm referring to those concerned; the others merely abide. I think we have a lot of followers. They are not certified copies; it's a state of mind which has been completely recuperated and integrated. I believe we invented a style, and I say that without any pretensions but with a great deal of lucidity. We didn't feel any of the consequences of our style. We never had any strategy. I think that we probably need a more commercially-minded third person. For several years, I've had the idea of structuring our work like a business, in other words, making Garouste & Bonetti into a brand name and a label with different ranges of products. I'm doing less drafting these days, and much more calculating. People take us for fools because even after twenty years now, we still haven't got business cards, we have never sent a bill on letter-head paper, nor have we ever had a secretary. We need to answer the telephone because we custom-make furniture to size. Our work is similar to a fashion designer's: the customer feels treated in a privileged fashion.

L: You were saying for instance that you could produce objects which would cost one-hundred-fifty dollars and yet look like they cost fifteen-

hundred and vice versa. Is that related to kitsch at all?

E: It involves a certain detachment with regard to the idea of a make and a signature. Making objects with poor materials ends up being relatively expensive because we spend a lot of time at it; but it does produce an interesting confusion of issues. The person who buys the piece also takes a certain risk because for whoever goes into their living room, there is no way of telling if they built the piece themselves: there is no sign of a make, nor of money, nor of material. It's a way of gently perverting the market. But in my opinion, it has nothing to do with kitsch. What does have to do with kitsch are certain pieces such as the *Turtle* which are deliberately done in 'bad taste'. In our case, the use of figurative elements leads to flirting with kitsch. A lighter-holder at five hundred dollars to hold a two-dollar object is outrageously kitsch.

L: Elizabeth, do you have any questions you might like to ask Mattia?

E: That's a People-type question. I'd prefer not to know.

M: She knows everything!

E: Not quite, fortunately!

L: Mattia, do you have any questions for Elizabeth?

E: He knows everything! Do you believe in God, Mattia? I believe we have a great deal of modesty. We're not extroverts. There are many things which remain unsaid. A partnership such as ours can only last as long as it has because there is a certain amount of restraint. Each to his or her own realm and family.

M: I guess that even in married couples, there are hidden domains! I'm off to Cadaques. Thank God! It's hard to get to!

Élizabeth Garouste

Élizabeth Garouste (née Rochline) studied interior architecture at the Ecole Camondo, Paris. She designed stage sets and costumes for Jean-Michel Ribes, and worked in fashion business. She works in partnership with Mattia Bonetti since 1981. She lives with her husband, painter Gérard Garouste, and their two children in Marcilly-sur-Eure and Paris.

Mattia Bonetti

Mattia Bonetti was born in 1952 in Lugano, Switzerland. He received his formal training as a textile designer at the Centro Scolastico per l'Industria Artistica in Lugano. He subsequently worked as a textile designer and photograph artist. He lives in Paris with his wife and two children.

1980

Gérard and Elizabeth Garouste are commissioned to design the Privilège club in a Paris discotheque and invite Mattia Bonetti to join them on the project, which marks the beginning of the partnership between Elisabeth Garouste and Mattia Bonetti.

1981

Make their debut as a design team with the "Barbare" collection shown at the Jansen house of interior design in Paris, an event which immediately gets them dubbed "les nouveaux barbares". Among the objects featured at the show is the *Chaise barbare*, the *Tripode* lamp and the *Cariatide* table.

1982

First collaboration with ORK Editions (which will subsequently take the name "En Attendant les Barbares")

1984

Begin to work with Paris-based editors Neotu.

1987

Found BGH Editions with Claude Hass.

1988

Begin working with the David Gill gallery in London.

Garouste & Bonetti work together with the following companies: Daum, Faïenceries de Gien and Molin, WMF, Swarovski, Roset, Bros's, Etamine, Rohleder, Habitat, Sam Laïk, Tapis Tisca, Saint-Jean d'Aubusson, Nina Ricci, Ricard and Christian Lacroix.

Color Photographs Index

1: *Turtle* ashtray (Blend Collection) 1995
Earthenware, hand painted in 36 different colours, 20x13x14 cm
Made by Gien, France.
Ed. Poeform (Stockholm)

2/3: Flat in Paris, 1998
Girl's room.
Phot. : Sylvain Thomas for Résidences Décoration

4: *Jalousie* cabinet, 1996
Darkened and gilded with a gold leaf metal, 140x130x50 cm
Ed. Neotu (Paris)
Phot : Neotu

5: *Aladin*, sofa, 1995
Bronze feet; black velvet appliqué on yellow silk, 180x100x110 cm
Ed. Genius (Italy)

6: *Koala* daybed, 1995
Bronze feet, 160x90x110cm
B.G.H. Éditions (Paris)

7: *Maharadjah*, sofa, 1990
'Snow' linen, pale blue silk velvet and silver plated bronze, 214x105x90 cm
Ed. Neotu (Paris)
Phot : Neotu

8: *Taormine*, bench seat, 1992
Patinated wrought iron, silk, embroidery and gilded bronze, 83x195x85 cm
Ed. Neotu (Paris)
Phot : Karin Knoblich

9: *Nomade* collection for the 3 Suisses catalogue, Fall-Winter 98-99
Foldable tent; sofa bed; hanging wardrobe; portable-lamp; puzzle-carpet.
Phot : Jean-Marc Palisse

10: *Prince Impérial*, chair, 1985
Painted wood and branches, raffia, 125x45x48 cm
Ed. Neotu (Paris)
Phot : Karin Knoblich

11: "Les Belles de Ricci", toilet water bottle, glass with metallic stopper, Nina Ricci, 1996

12: *Premium*, ceramic bottle for Ricard, 1998
Agent Kréo

13: (from left to right)
Column Elliniki, 1996
Black and white terracotta on bronze base, 169x60x60 cm
Column Love, 1996
Black terracotta with gold leaf on bronze base, 123x60x60 cm
Column Alhidia, 1996
Red and black terracotta on bronze base, 183x60x60 cm
Ed. David Gill gallery (London)

14: *Boogie Woogie* vase, 1997
Ceramic, enamels, metallic cover (gold or platinum), 45x53 cm
Ed. Néotu (Paris)

15/19: House P. S. Woo in Hong Kong, China, 1993-1996
15 : Entrance gate:
Patinated wrought iron, painted and gilded with gold leaf.
Bench seat : wengé wood, gilded wrought iron and bronze, covered with silk velvet tapestry.
Wall and floor: "Nuvolato" Carrare marble.
Phot : Antoine Bootz (courtesy of Nest).

16 : Guest room:
Walls with hand painted and gilded peony patterns from drawings by B. G.. Wrought iron bed; satin silk with appliqué works bed spread, bed head and cushion; wall console in black and golden patinated bronze; lacquered wood and wrought iron bedside table; iron lamp with pleated silk lampshade; hand painted and gilded sliding doors ; painting (oil on canvas by Francesco Clemente) lacquered and golden wood frame with golden wrought iron fasteners.
Phot : Antoine Bootz (courtesy of Nest).

17 : Grand salon, partial view:
Walls with hand painted and gilded peony patterns from drawings by B. G.; embroided wih golden threads silk curtains by the Lesage House; squat armchair covered with bronze and fabric fringe; side-table, bronze and marble sofa ; black and silver plated patinated bronze lamp (on the table), silk lampshade with silver plated bronze pendants; big wooden torchère, wrought iron and gilded with a white gold/ yellow gold leaf bronze; polished bronze standard lamp with sunshade shaped silk lampshade ; golden polished bronze pouf with embroided tapestry; golden wrought iron console table with marble top; marble-like painted wood mirror with golden bronze appliqué works and fasteners.
Phot : Antoine Bootz (courtesy of Nest).

18 : Lounge from the guest room :
Walls with hand painted and gilded chinoiserie patterns from drawings by B.G.; low armless chair and sofa covered with buttoned velvet on a black patinated bronze bamboo-like structure; bronze lamp, silk lampshade; wrought iron standard lamp with pleated silk lampshade trimmed with small onyx pearls.
Phot : Antoine Bootz (courtesy of Nest).

19: Playing room, partial view
Woollen carpet from the Saint-Jean d'Aubusson manufacture; golden wrought iron small armchairs with leather covers; wengé wood table with leather-covered top; sofa-bed covered with cotton printed with Fortuny; golden wrought iron and lacquered wood bedside tables; bronze lamp, silk lampshade.
Phot : Antoine Bootz (courtesy of Nest).

20: *Sputnik* lamp, 1994
Limoges enamel,44x21 cm
Ed. BG

21: Bottles for the Nina Ricci cosmetics collection "Deci Delà", 1994

22 : *Cathédrale* cupboard, 1988
Lacquered wood and metal, blown and straightened glass, 160x80x40 cm
Ed. Neotu (Paris)
Phot: Karin Knoblich

23: Inside view of the Montpellier tramway, 1998
Computer-generated image by Deis, Paris.
Agent Kreo

24: Schlesinger House, London, 1996
View of the living-room and of the dining-room.
Living-room: tufted wool carpet; silk covered sofa, gilded with a gold leaf bronze foot; sofa 'duchesse brisée' upholstered with leopard printed velvet; golden wrought iron small table, gilded terracotta top.
Dining-room: hand-tufted wool carpet with bronze inlays, golden Wengé wood chairs covered with velvet; golden wengé wood table with wengé top; blown glass and golden wrought iron chandelier.
Phot : Thierry Jeanson (courtesy of Inside Stock Image).

1 ◀

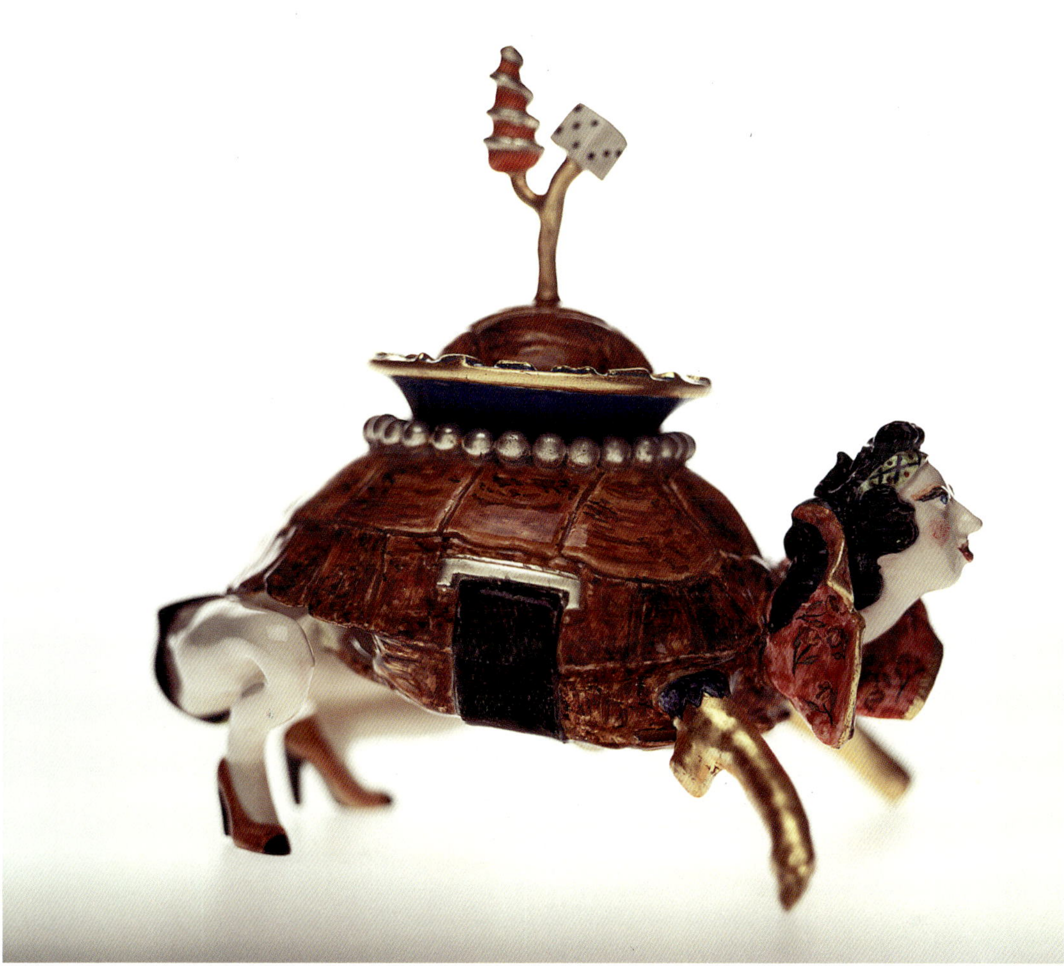

2 ▶

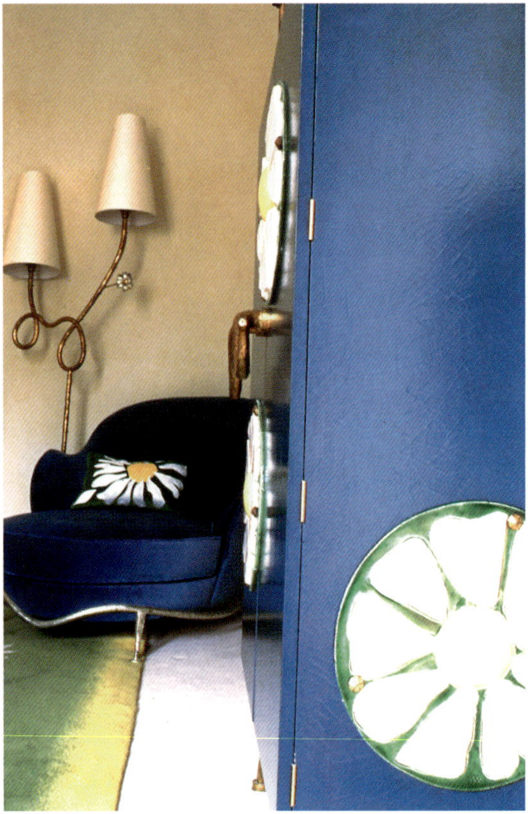

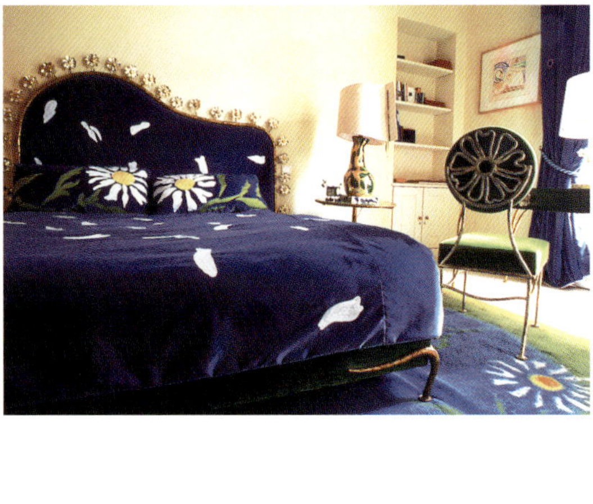

3 ▶

4 ◀

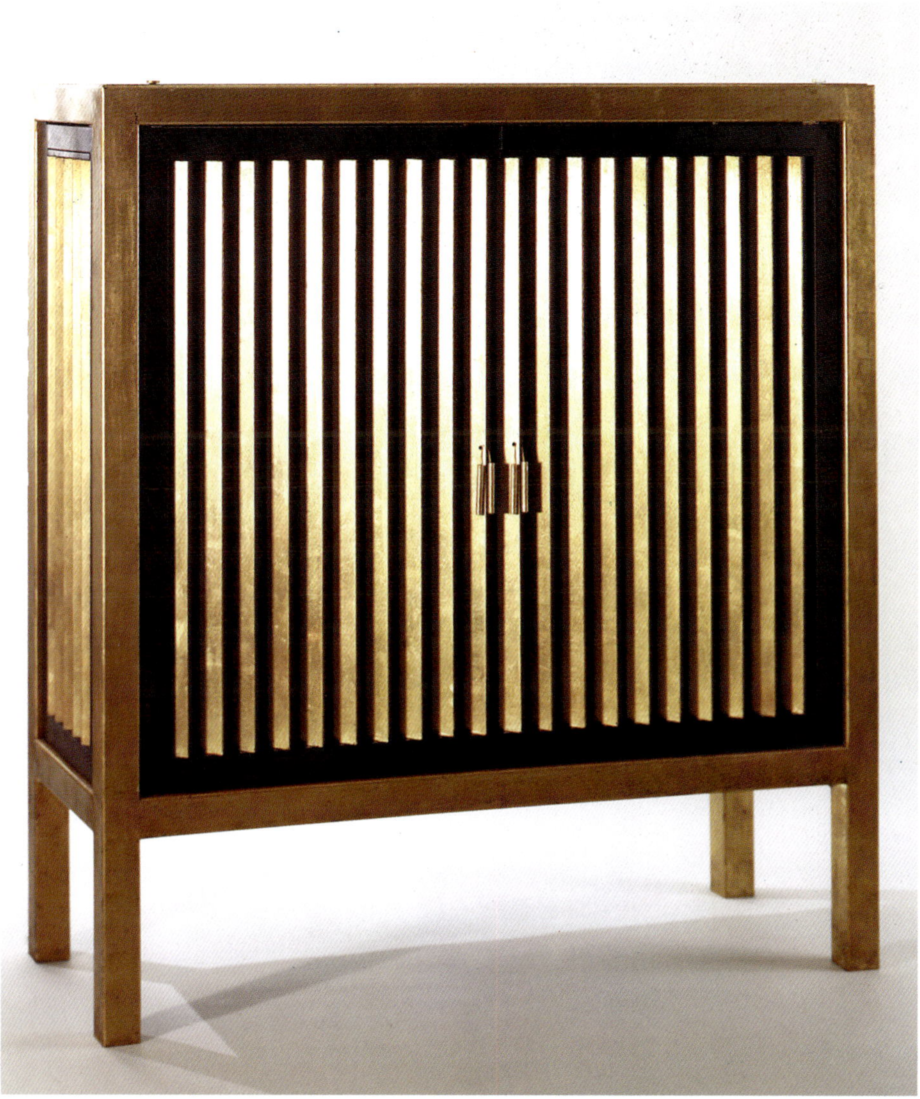

5 ▶

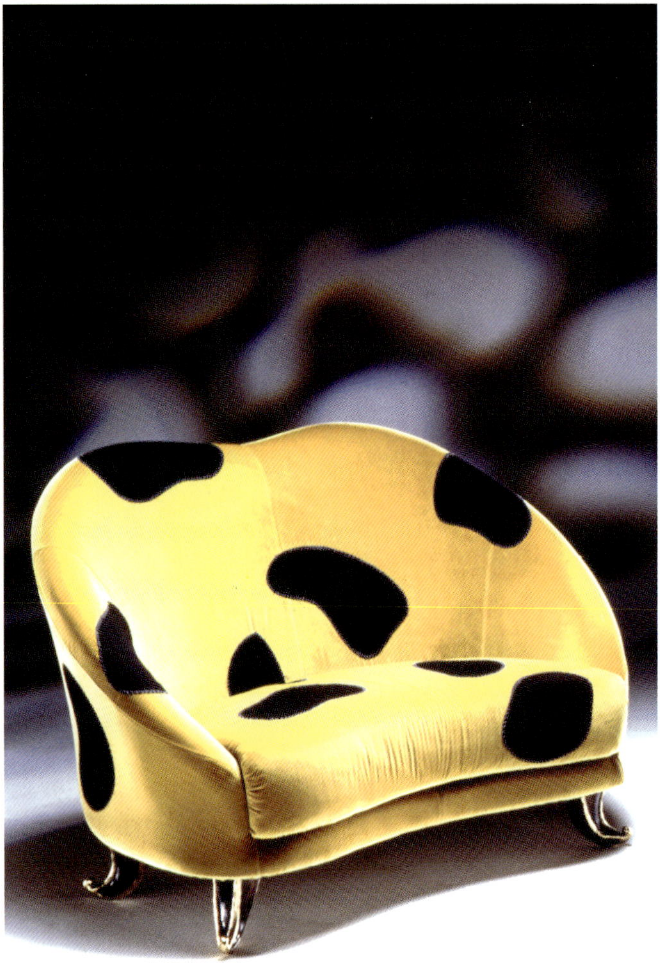

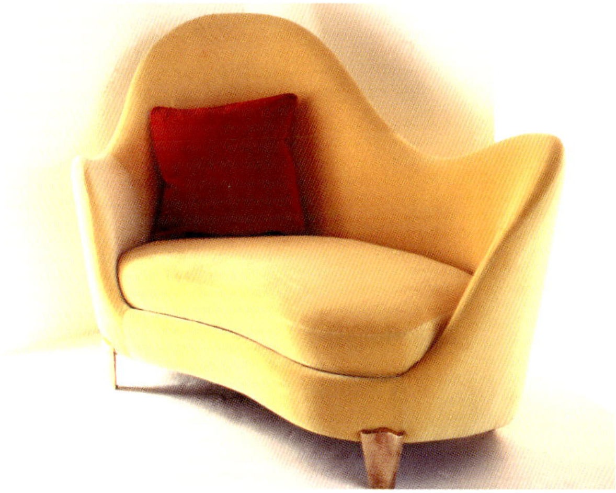

6 ◀

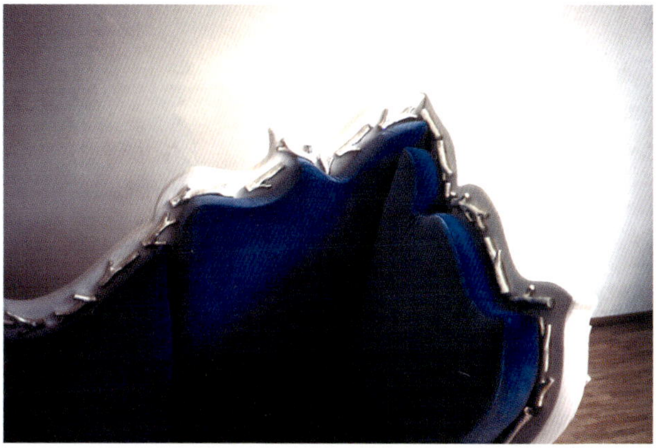

7 ◀

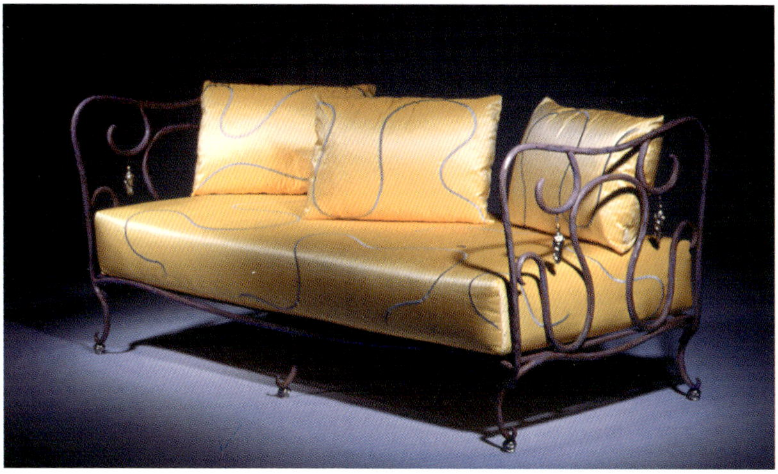

8 ◀

9 ▼

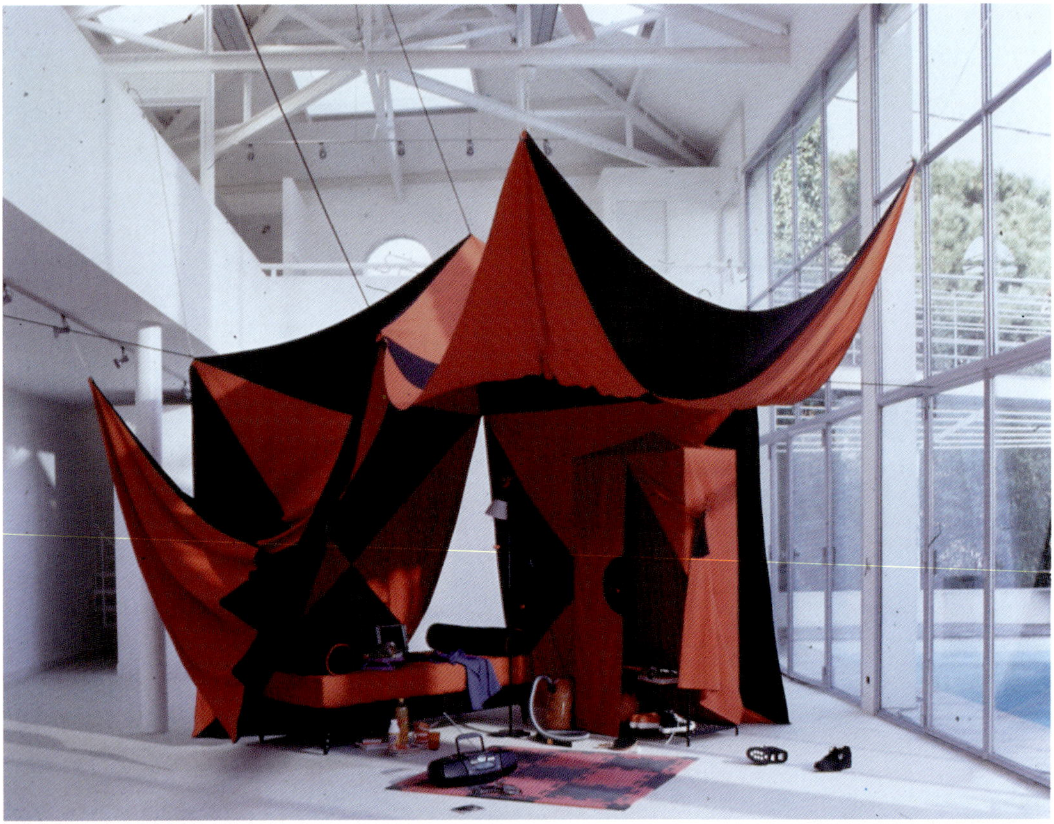

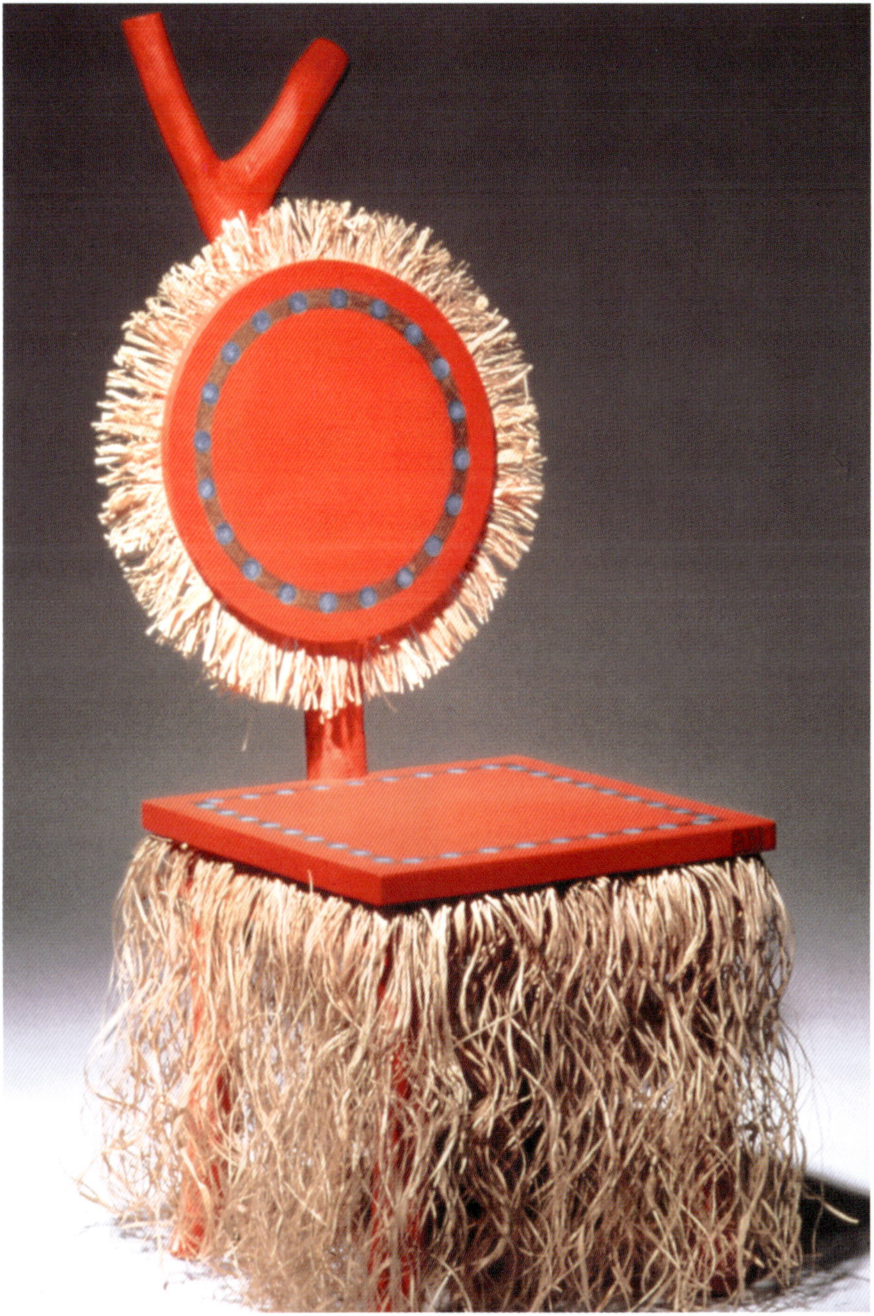

10 ◀

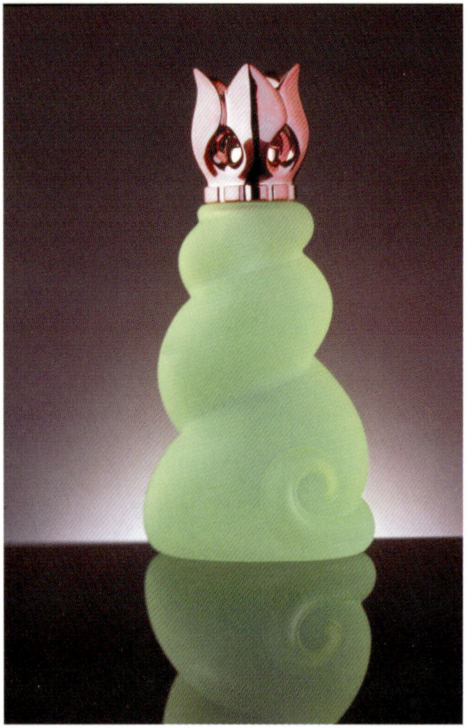

11 ▲

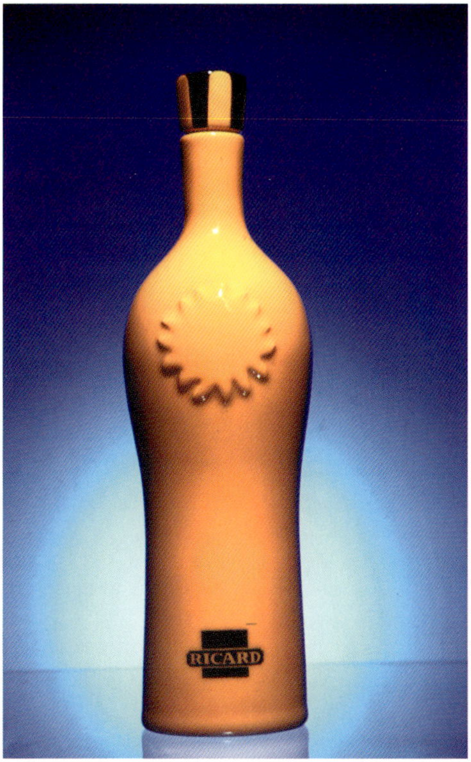

12 ▶

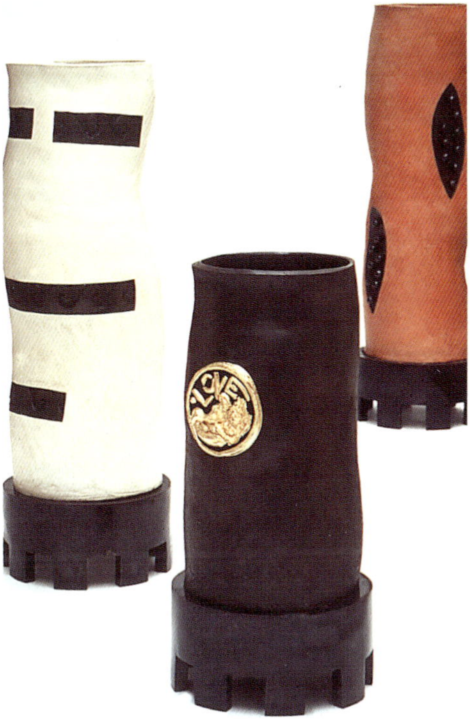

13 ◄

14 ▼

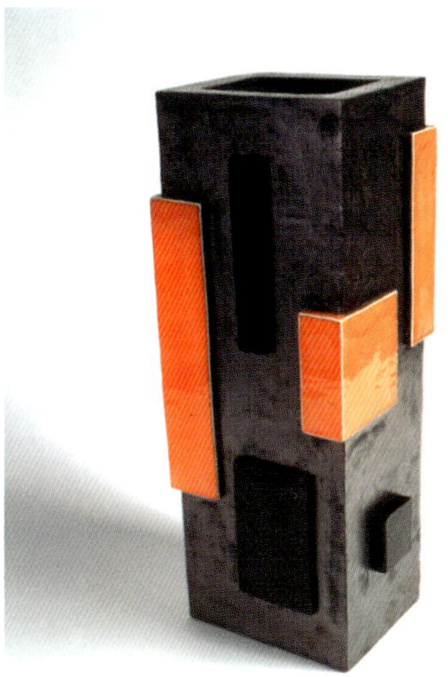

15 ►►

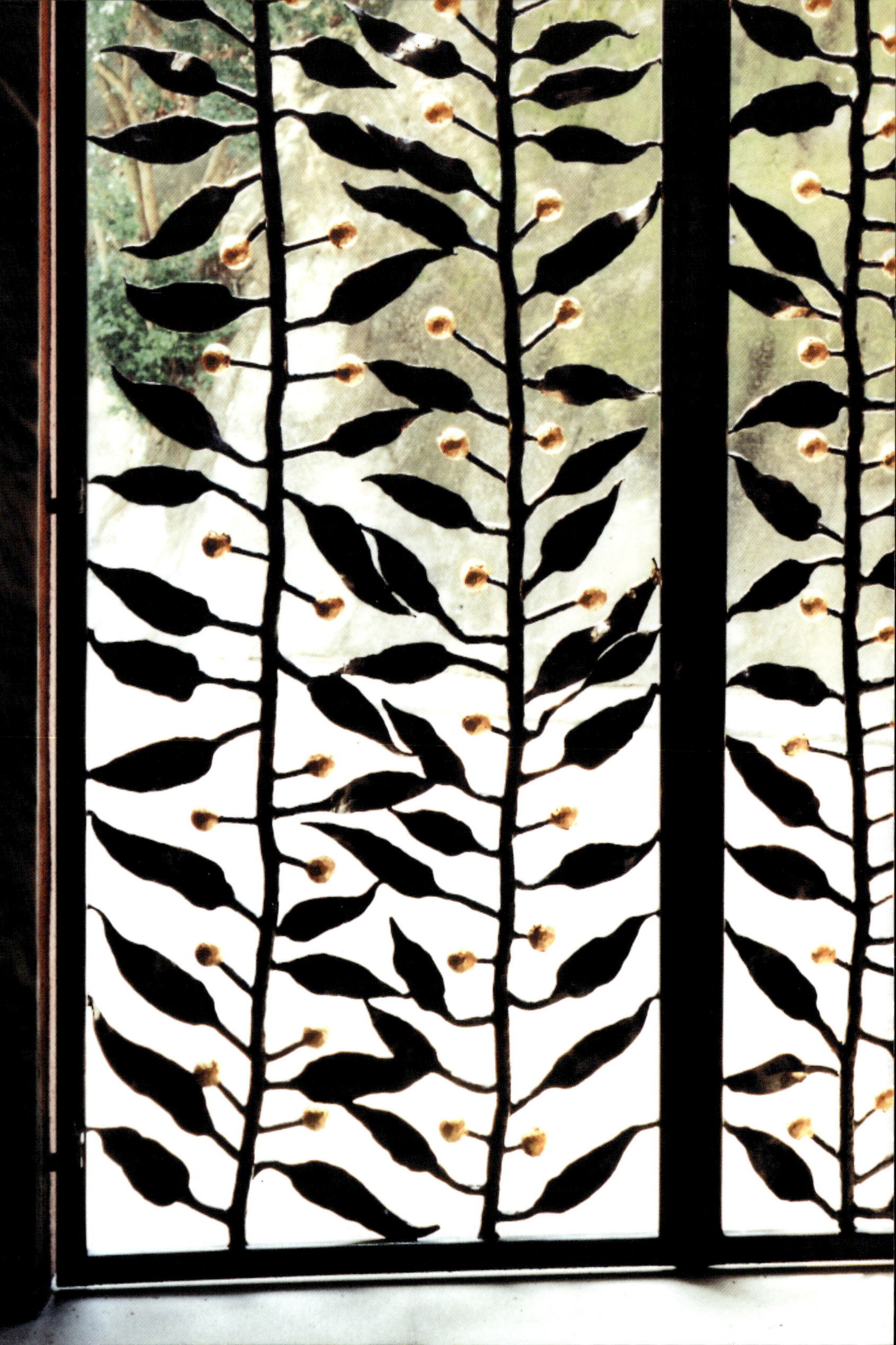

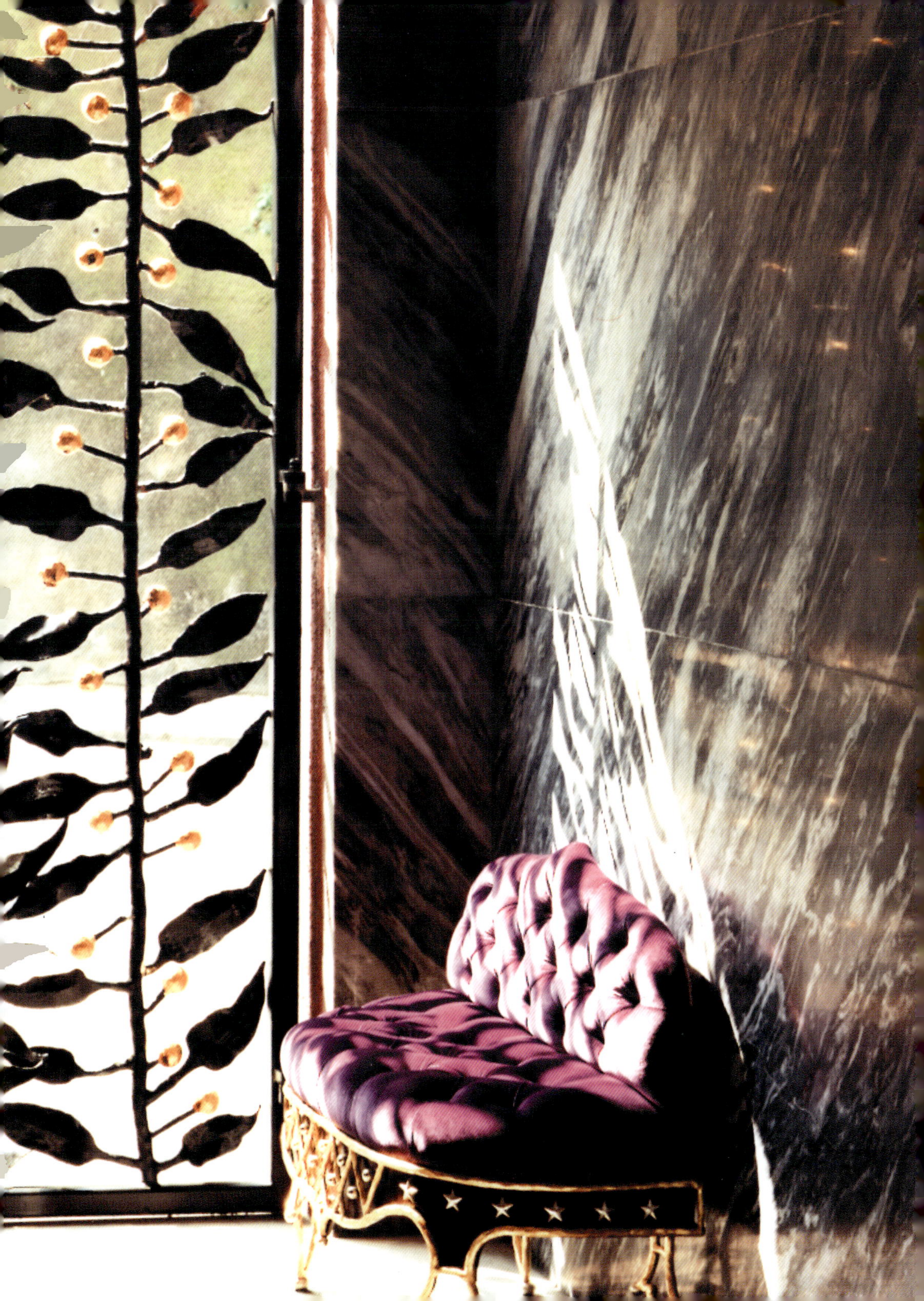

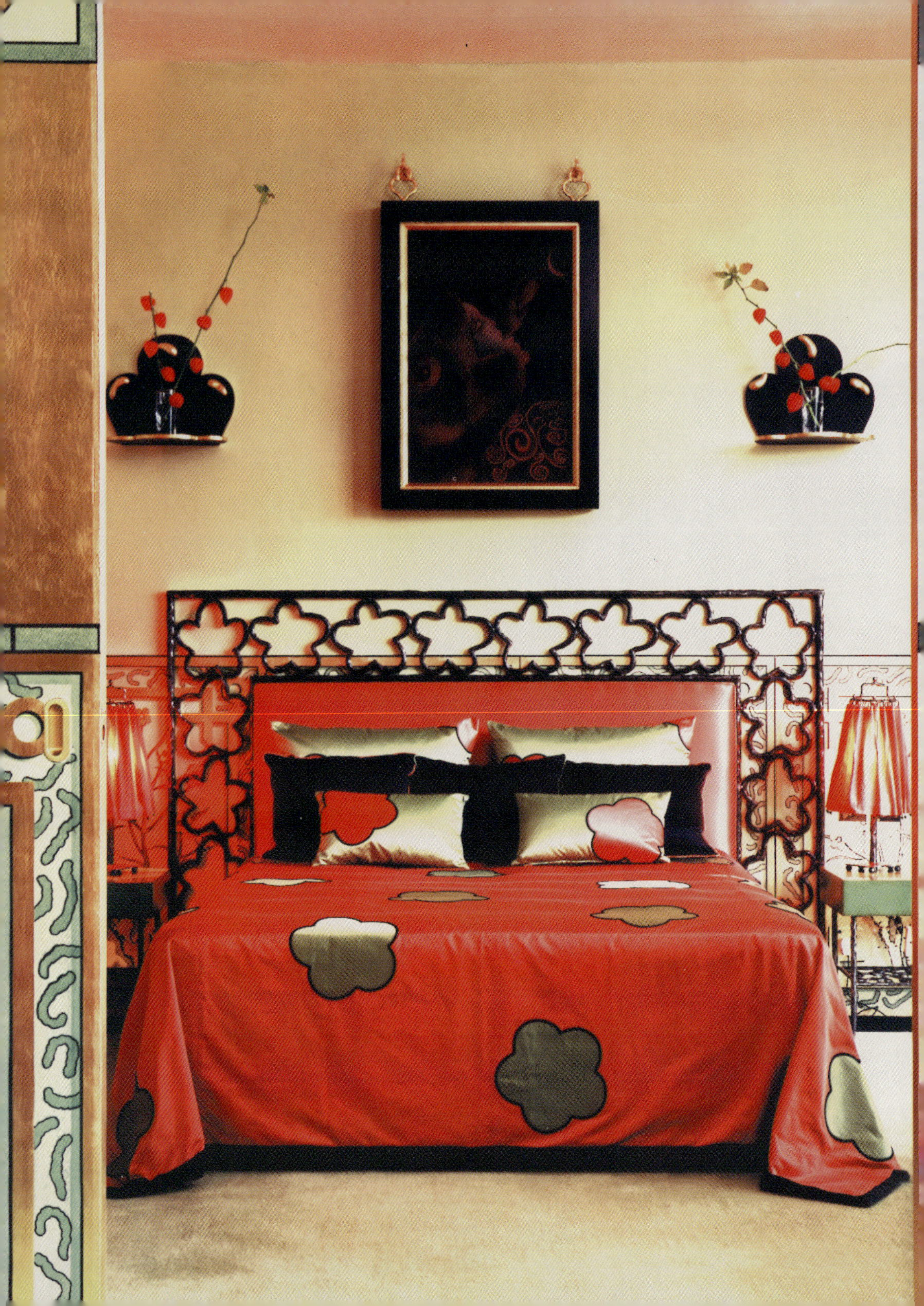

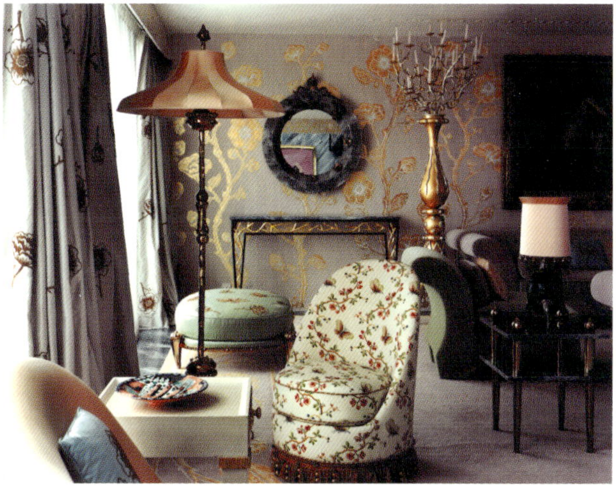

16 ◀◀

17 ◀

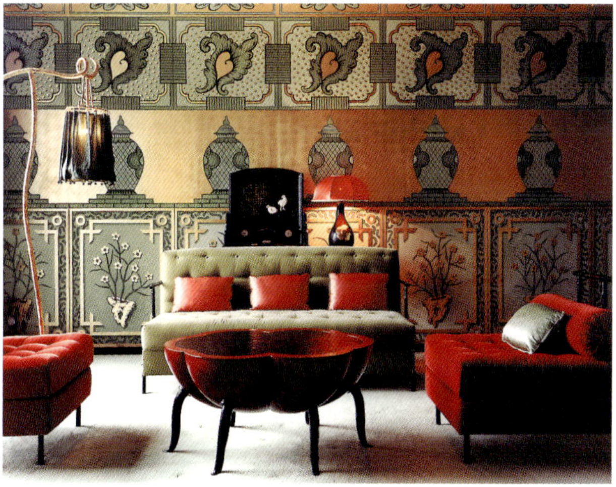

18 ◀

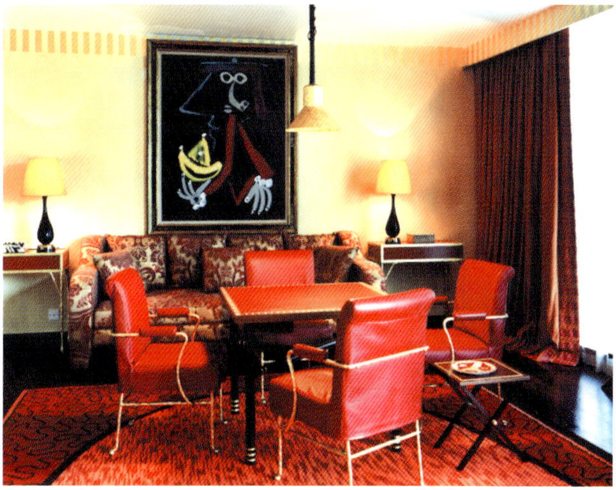

19 ◀

20 ▶

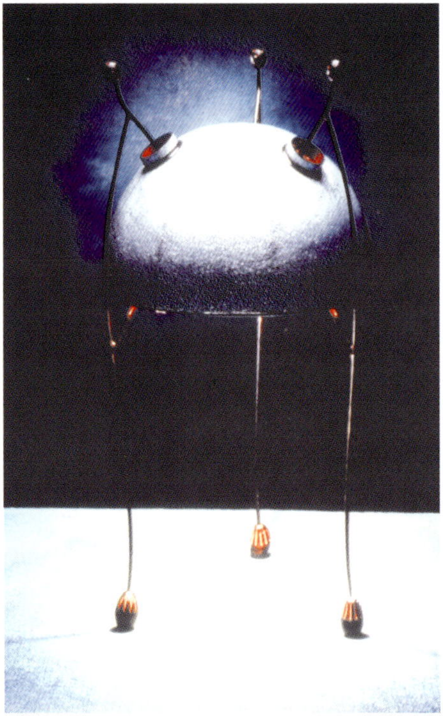

21 ▼

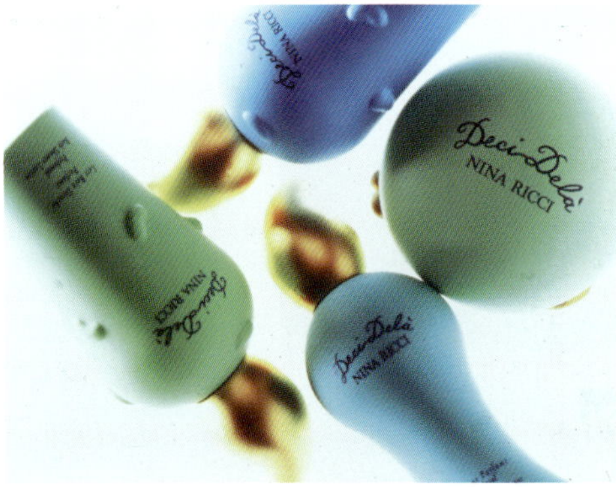

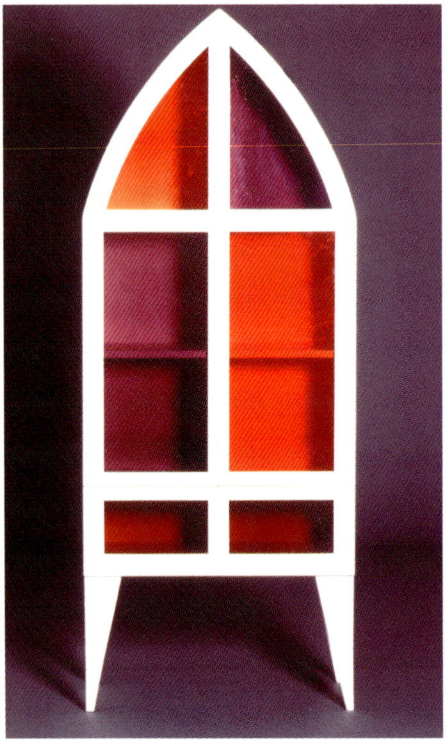

22 ▲

23 ▼

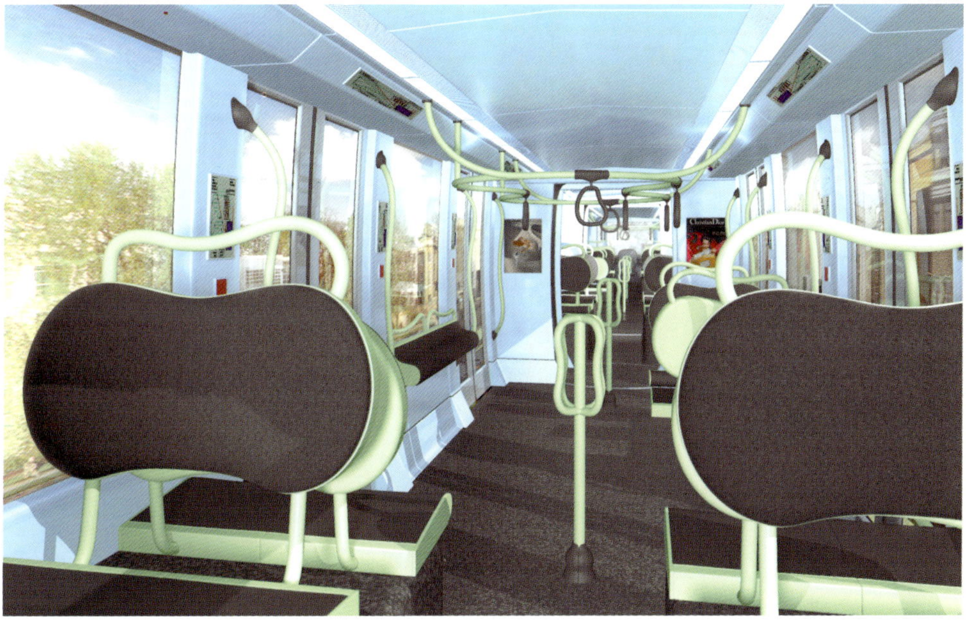

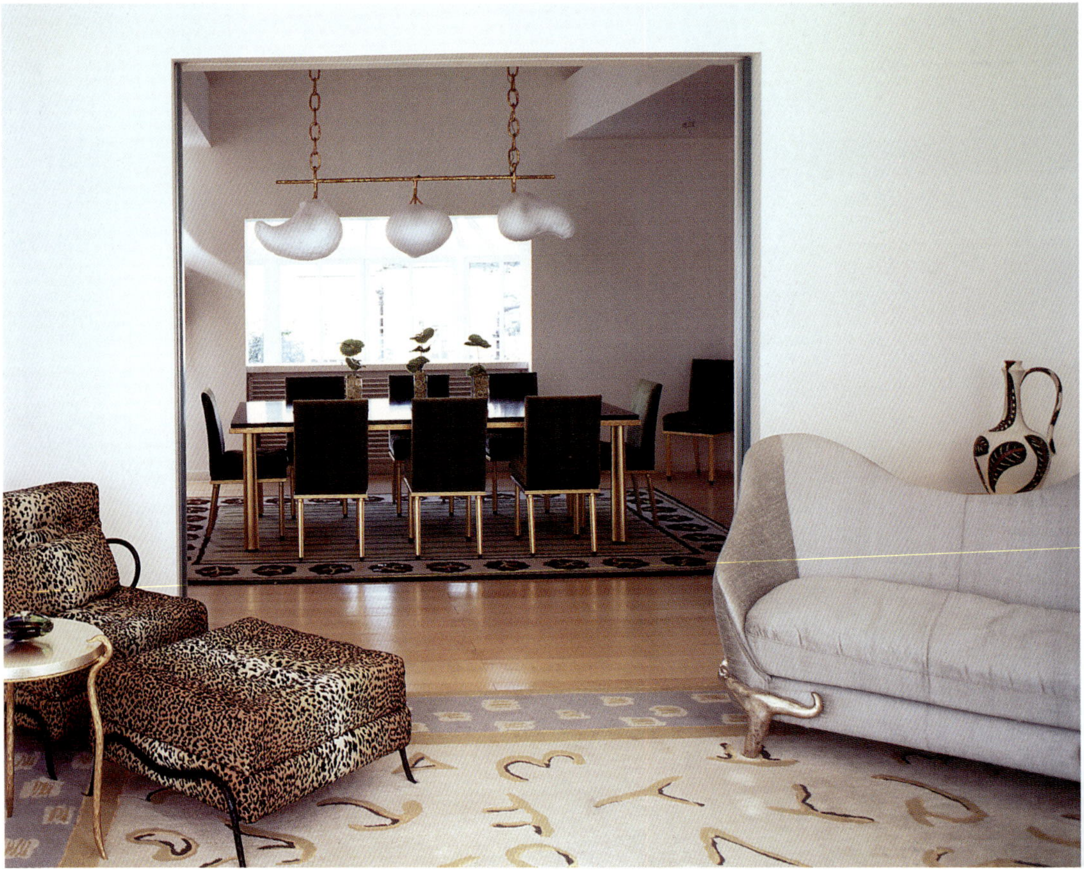

Furniture & Product Design

1980

BG Editions, Paris:
Barbare chair

1982

BG Editions, Paris:
Rocher table and bench

1983

BG Editions, Paris:
Menhir console table

1984

ORK, Paris:
Masque lamp

Neotu, Paris:
Grande Ourse collection (mirror, lamp and carpet)

1985

Néotu, Paris:
Prince Imperial chair and table.

1986

Neotu, Paris:
Terracotta Cabinet (by Elizabeth Garouste)

1988

Neotu, Paris:
Maharadja (sofa), *Tam-Tam* (standard lamp), *Cathedral* cabinet, *Arc-en-ciel* table, *Dogon* armchair and *Fersen* chest.

1989

BGH Editions, Paris
"Patchwork" collection

Daum and Lieux Editions, Paris
"Trapani" collection (glassware, tableware, flatware, furniture, lamps, mirrors)

1990

Lou Fagotin, Saint Pierre de Fursac, France
"ISBA" collection (chair and table, joined in 1992, by a chest and wall applique made from hazel branches) presented at the Paris Furniture Fair

Neotu, Paris
Belgravia chest, *Rodeo* (armchair and table), bronze bed *Beaux Rêves*

Sam Laïk Editions, Paris
Collection of carpets

En Attendant les Barbares, Paris
Collection of furniture and objects in wrought iron and bronze

BGH Editions, Paris
Mars (sofa)

1991

Eva Maria Melchers, Bremen, Germany
Petite Etoile and *Petit Nuage* (tables)

1992

Nina Ricci
Design "Le Teint Ricci" series of flacons and packaging, for which they are awarded the "Prix d'excellence de la création"

Best Friends, Bad-Essen, Germany
Jewellery collection (necklaces, rings, earrings, brooches)

1993

Liberty, London
Collection of oak furniture in the spirit of the Arts and Crafts tradition

1994

WMF, Germany
Tableware

Nina Ricci
Flacon design and packaging for cosmetics series "Deci-Delà"

Ricard (pastis producer)
Design of a carafe

David Gill, London
Flowers in the Wood cabinet, *Kawabuko* chest of drawers,
You and Me double table, *S/M* armchair

Blome, Sundern, Germany
Collection of curtain rods

1995/1997
Design of a furniture group for Mobilier National

1996

Nina Ricci
New flacon design and packaging: "Les Belles de Ricci"

Feodora Fastabend, Germany
Furnitures for hotels

Carte Noire
Packaging and sleeve for freeze-dried coffee

1998
Furniture design for the Fall-Winter 98-99 catalogue of "Les 3 Suisses"

Interior Design/Public spaces

1980

Gérard and Elizabeth Garouste are commissioned to design the Privilège club in Le Palace, a Paris discotheque and invite Mattia Bonetti to join them on the project.

1987

Are retained by Christian Lacroix to do the interior design at his Haute Couture salon in the rue du Faubourg Saint-Honoré, Paris. Also design the interior of the Géopoly restaurant in the rue du Faubourg Montmartre, Paris.

1988

Design and furnish the residential quarters of Bernard Picasso at the castle of Boisgeloup, France.

Staging of the exhibition "Vraiment faux" at the Cartier Foundation, Jouy-en-Josas, France (the exhibition was shown again in 1990 in Milan and Munich).

1989

Design of the private quarters of Princess Gloria von Thurn und Taxis in Regensburg, Germany.

1990

Design of the interior of the Schloßcafé in Regensburg, and the entrance pavilion for the museum of Regensburg, Germany.

1991

Interior design and decoration of privately owned residences in Germany and the UK

Design of the salons privés of the Banque Bruxelles Lambert in Geneva.

1992

Interior design of the of Mr P.S. Woo's residence in Hong Kong.

Together with five other designers, Garouste & Bonetti participate, with their *Dreaming Room* installation, in the "Ambiente Electronica" project sponsored by Philips Consumer Electronics, in Berlin, Germany.

1994

Design of the "Hommage à Max Jacob" footbridge for the town of Quimper, France.

1995

Various interior design commissions for residences in the UK, Greece, France, and for a yacht.

1996

Interior design of the restaurant Strozzi's in Zürich, Switzerland.

1997

Interior design of the Aristoff cigars shop in Beverly Hills, USA.

1998

Design of the Montpellier tramway, France.

Furniture design for the Foyer of the Royal Theatre of Namur, Belgium.

Selected exhibitions

1980

Solo exhibition at the Jansen gallery, Paris.

1982

Solo exhibition at the Furniture of the Twentieth Century gallery, New York.

1984

Exhibition at the V.I.A. gallery in Paris.

1985

Solo exhibition at the Musée des Arts Décoratifs, Bordeaux, France.

Exhibit at the following shows: "Vivre en couleurs," staged by the Fondation Cartier, "Suzanne est au salon" at the Musée des Beaux Arts, Dunkerque, "Les Cafés littéraires" in Paris and Rome.

1986

Group exhibition "Wohnen von Sinnen", at the Kunstmuseum, Düsseldorf

Exhibitions at galleries Shiseido, Tokyo, and Neotu, Paris and the Venice Biennal.

1987

Solo exhibition at the city hall of Villeurbane, Lyon, France.

1988

Group exhibitions: "The Most Contemporary French Design" at the Victoria and Albert Museum, London, "V.I.A. et la Révolution," Grande Halle de la Villette, Paris, and "Design français 1960-1990: trois décennies," Centre Georges Pompidou, Paris.

Individual exhibitions at the David Gill gallery in London and Neotu, Paris.

1989

Group exhibition at the Tel-Aviv-Museum, Israel.

Individual exhibitions at the David Gill gallery in London and Seibu gallery, Tokyo.

1990

Group exhibitions: “10 ans du V.I.A.,” Musée des Arts Décoratifs, Paris.

Individual exhibitions at the following galleries: Neotu, Paris and New York, Wunderhaus, Munich, Ex-Ante, Rome.

1991

Individual exhibitions: Grands Magasins du Printemps, Paris, and at galleries Alcazar, Milan, En attendant les Barbares, Paris, Colonna, Hannover.

1993

Group exhibition: “French Designers' Show House,” New York.

Individual exhibitions at galleries Neotu, Paris and New York, Naîla de Monbrison, Paris, Wohngalerie Tendenz, Innsbruck, and at the Musée F. Mandet, Riom.

1994

Individual exhibitions at galleries Neotu, Paris, David Gill, London and at the Arts Centre of Sundern, Germany.

1996

Solo exhibitions at the Centre d'Art Contemporain de Maymac, France, at the Pauline Karpidas Foundation, Hydra, Greece and at the Neotu gallery, Paris.

1997

Group exhibitions: “Design français” at Boulogne Billancourt, France, “Des jardins à vivre”, Le Limousin, France.

Individual exhibition at the Centre Georges Pompidou, CCI, Paris.

1998

Group exhibition: “Premices: Invested spaces in visual arts, architecture and design from France 1958-1998” at the Guggenheim Museum, New York.

Solo exhibition at the David Gill gallery, London.

Bibliography

Stephen Calloway, François Baudot, Gérard-George Lemaire, *Elizabeth Garouste et Mattia Bonetti* , Michel Aveline Ed., Marseille 1990

Volker Albus, Stephen Calloway, Raymond Guidot, Suzanne Slesin, Sophie Tasma Anargyros, *Garouste & Bonetti*, Verlag Form GmbH, Frankfurt am Main, 1996

Also available from Dis Voir

PLASTIC ARTS

LITERATURE/FINE ART/CINEMA

Raúl Ruiz
Poetics of Cinema
The Book of Disappearances & The Book of Tractations
A la Poursuite de l'Ile au Trésor

Peter Greenaway
The Falls
Rosa
Fear of Drowning by Numbers
Papers - (Paintings, Collages and Drawings)
The Draughtsman's Contract
A Zed & Two Noughts
The Belly of an Architect
Drowning by Numbers
The Cook, the Thief, his Wife and her Lover
The Baby of Mâcon
The Pillow Book

Manoel de Oliveira
Angelica
Lisbonne Culturelle
Les Cannibales

CINEMA

Jean-Marc Lalanne, Ackbar Abbas, David Martinez, Jimmy Ngai
Wong Kar-wai

Paul Virilio, Carole Desbarats, Jacinto Lageira, Danièle Rivière
Atom Egoyan

Michael Nyman, Daniel Caux, Michel Field, Florence de Mèredieu, Philippe Pilard
Peter Greenaway

Christine Buci-Glucksmann, Fabrice Revault d'Allonnes
Raúl Ruiz

Yann Lardeau, Jacques Parsi, Philippe Tancelin
Manoel de Oliveira

CHOREOGRAPHY

Paul Virilio, René Thom, Laurence Louppe, Jean-Noël Laurenti, Valérie Preston-Dunlop

Traces of Dance - Drawings and Notations of Choreographers

ARCHITECTURE

Christian de Portzamparc

Genealogy of Forms

DESIGN

Pierre Staudenmayer, Nadia Croquet, Laurent Le Bon

Élizabeth Garouste & Mattia Bonetti

Philippe Louguet, Dagmar Sedlincká

Borek Sìpek

Raymond Guidot, Olivier Boissière

Ron Arad

François Burkhardt, Cristina Morozzi

Andrea Branzi

ÉDITIONS DIS VOIR: 3, RUE BEAUTREILLIS - F-75004 PARIS
PHONE (33 - 1) 48 87 07 09 - FAX (33 - 1) 48 87 07 14
e-mail: DISVOIR@AOL.com